SCOTTISH BALLADS

Edited and Introduced by
Emily Lyle

CANONGATE
CLASSICS

55

First published in 1994 by Canongate Press Ltd, 14
Frederick Street, Edinburgh EH2 2HB.Introduction and
Notes © Emily Lyle 1994.

The editor is most grateful to the following for permission
to reproduce the ballads listed: to Aberdeen University
Library for No 32; to Aberdeen University Studies for Nos
4, 5, 47, 52 and 60; to Kenneth Goldstein for the fragment
of 'The Baron of Brackley' in the introduction; to The
Crawford (Bibliotheca Lindesiana) Collections placed on
deposit in The National Library of Scotland for No 11; to
The School of Scottish Studies, University of Edinburgh,
for Nos 9, 10, 66 and 78; and to The Scottish Text Society
for Nos 17, 18, 27, 67, 68, 76, 77 and 83.

British Library Cataloguing-in-Publication Data
A catalogue record for this book is available on request
from the British Library.

ISBN 0 86241 477 6

The publishers gratefully acknowledge general subsidy
from the Scottish Arts Council towards the Canongate
Classics series and a specific grant towards
the publication of this title.

Set in Plantin by Advance, Edinburgh.
Printed and bound in Finland by WSOY.

Contents

	Introduction	9
	Note on Language and Sources	23
1	The Battle of Otterburn	27
2	Kinmont Willie	32
3	Johnie Armstrang	39
4	The Battle o' Harlaw	44
5	Johnnie o' Braidiesleys	48
6	Sir Patrick Spens	50
7	The Bonny Earl of Murray	54
8	Edom of Gordon	55
9	The Bonnie Hoose o Airlie	59
10	The Baron of Brackley	61
11	The Gaberlunzie-Man	62
12	Donald of the Isles	65
13	Johny Faa, the Gypsy Laddie	68
14	The Gowans Sae Gay	70
15	The Wind Hath Blown My Plaid Away	71
16	The Earl of Rosslyn's Daughter	73
17	The Unco Knicht's Wouing	76
18	The Fause Knicht	78
19	The Daemon Lover	79
20	Burd Ellen	81
21	The Place Where My Love Johnny Dwells	86
22	Young Bicham	88
23	Hind Horn	91
24	Katharine Jaffray	94

25	Lord Thomas and Fair Annie	96
26	Wee Messgrove	100
27	Bob Norris	105
28	Lord Thomas and Fair Annet	108
29	The Twa Sisters	113
30	Sweet William's Ghost	115
31	The Wife of Usher's Well	118
32	The Maid of Coldingham	120
33	Clark Colven	122
34	The Great Silkie of Sule Skerry	124
35	Tam Lin	125
36	Thomas the Rhymer	132
37	King Orpheus	135
38	Sir Colin	137
39	The Twa Magicians	140
40	The Broomfield Hill	142
41	Gil Brenton	144
42	The Broom of Cowdenknows	151
43	The Shepherd's Dochter	155
44	The Shepherd's Son	160
45	The Earl of Errol	162
46	Lord Jamie Douglas	164
47	The Laird o' Drum	166
48	The Cooper of Fife	170
49	Get Up and Bar the Door	171
50	Our Goodman	173
51	The Farmer's Curst Wife	177
52	Bog o' Gight	178
53	The Laird o Logie	182
54	Johnie Scott	184
55	Lang Johnny Moir	188
56	The Keach i the Creel	195
57	The Gay Goss Hawk	198
58	Love Gregor	202
59	The Drowned Lovers	206
60	The Dowie Dens o' Yarrow	211

61	The Douglas Tragedy	213
62	Clerk Sanders	216
63	Lady Maisry	220
64	The Broom o the Cathery Knowes	224
65	The Cruel Brother	226
66	Son David	229
67	Rosianne	230
68	Lady Jean	233
69	The Broom Blooms Bonnie and Says It Is Fair	236
70	The High Banks o Yarrow	237
71	Willie's Lady	239
72	Lamkin	242
73	The Jew's Daughter	246
74	The Cruel Mother	248
75	Marie Hamilton	250
76	Earl Richard	252
77	Lord Thomas and Lady Margeret	255
78	Lord Ronald	257
79	Bonny Barbara Allan	258
80	The Blue Flowers and the Yellow	260
81	Glenlogie	261
82	The Twa Corbies	263
83	The Thrie Ravens	264
	Notes	266
	Index	285

Introduction

The oral tradition of the Scottish ballads has formed a unique strand in our cultural history. The ballads have made their mark on published literature too, for many writers, most notably Burns and Scott,[1] have drawn inspiration from them, and have been involved in their preservation — for these songs were rarely written down by those who sang them, and we depend instead on records of their performance made by collectors.[2]

Scottish ballads learnt orally are still being sung in the twentieth century and so in a sense they remain part of contemporary literature. But they are also regarded as 'old songs' and indeed they were already regarded in that way at the time of the first wave of collecting in the late eighteenth and early nineteenth century. Some oral genres, such as the short mythological songs of the Baltic region, are of extreme antiquity, but the Scottish ballads, although old, are not extremely old, for their rhymed verse form dates from the late Middle Ages. What *can* be extremely old about them is their content, since narratives and motifs pass from one genre to another. The riddle contest, for example, found in 'The Wind Hath Blown My Plaid Away', 'The Earl of Rosslyn's Daughter', 'The Unco Knicht's Wouing' and 'The Fause Knicht' is likely to go back to prehistory.

The earliest references in the ballads to historical characters or events are to the late thirteenth century — the time of the earliest named poet in Scots, Thomas of Erceldoune called the Rhymer, who lived in the reign of Alexander III and is the protagonist of 'Thomas the Rhymer'. Then there is 'Sir Patrick Spens' which bears some resemblance to the events of 1290 following the death of Alexander III. These ballads, however, are not known to exist before the eighteenth century, although there is a romance-prophecy of the fourteenth century called *Thomas of Erceldoune* which may embody parts of an earlier form of a ballad.[3] The earliest case included here of a ballad text nearly contemporary with the events it relates is 'Edom of Gordon' which occurs in a late sixteenth-century manuscript.[4]

When we try to understand the roots of the ballads as we have them, we must keep in mind how few records have survived even from more recent centuries. When we remember that a ballad could be sung by very many singers and could be sung by one singer on many occasions, we realise that what was picked up by collectors was only a small sample — like a bucketful from an ocean. Oral forms are always elusive, of course, but even written or printed records are mere remnants from a vaster stock, now lost. For example, many songs were printed on broadsides or in little pamphlets called chapbooks, and I turned over thousands and thousands of these in libraries on the look-out for a version of 'Tam Lin' without ever finding one. And then I was given a copy of an eighteenth-century chapbook containing it by a fellow scholar, Matthew McDiarmid, who had picked it up in a bookshop. Clearly, it was just a matter of chance that this copy survived, although a good many must have been printed. This example is far from being a unique case, for many chapbook and broadside versions of ballads are known in only one or two copies, like the version of 'The Gaberlunzie-Man' reprinted here for the first time. Because of the heavy loss of this ephemeral material, it can be assumed that there were many more ballads printed in chapbooks and broadsides which have not survived on paper. In short, we do not have the whole picture and are often reduced to guess-work.[5]

In some cases, however, the background to ballads from the eighteenth century onwards *has* been filled in by the discovery of earlier manuscript versions. One such case is a sixteenth-century manuscript text of 'Sir Colin', the discovery of which settled a dispute about whether or not the ballad had early Scottish roots. This is completely ballad-like in parts but it also uses recurrent rhyme which is not at all typical of the ballads. For example, the whole of the lady's speech to Sir Colin telling him of the adventure by which he may prove his worth and win her hand, and part of his reply, has a recurrent -orn rhyme:

> Scho sayis upone yone allreche hill
> Thairon standis ane thorn
> And ye wald walk ane winter nicht
> And baldlie blaw your horn
> Ane alreche knycht is mikill of mycht
> Will compeir yow biforne
> Thair com never ane away with lyf
> Sen the first tyme that I was borne
> Thair my hand said Sir Collyne
> I sall walk at that thorne
> Outher ane wad to bring away
> Or ellis my lyf to be forlorne[6]

When this feature of recurrent rhyme is lost, we have a simplified form contained within the four-line stanza, as in the case of the only use of the -orn rhyme in the later ballad version printed here ('Sir Colin', verse 8).

The normal verse for ballads is a four-line stanza with alternate four-stress and three-stress iambic lines rhyming abcb, and this is usually just called ballad metre. A regular example is verse 8 of 'The Battle of Otterburn':

> But O how pale his lady lookd,
>   Frae aff the castle-wa,
> When down before the Scottish spear
>   She saw proud Percy fa.

Not infrequently, the second and fourth lines are refrains, repeated each time when the ballad is sung, but not printed out in full. In fact, these lines give scope for audience participation in the singing of a ballad.

We should never forget that the ballad is a sung genre[7] with a whole musical dimension that is not caught by the printed text; to gain a full appreciation, every opportunity should be taken of listening to live or recorded performances.[8] Whatever efforts we make, however, we can never recapture contemporary singings of ballad versions from earlier centuries and it is useful, in thinking about this, to separate out the ideas of text and context.[9] The text can be caught in print and transferred bodily from one context to another and may have quite different purposes and effects in different contexts. For example, a singer may sing for his or her own satisfaction without anyone else being present, and can even perform silently in the mind. Then, when an audience *is* present, the experience may vary in a number of ways. One important variation is the degree to which singer and audience form part of the same milieu. If those listening to a singer are accustomed to hearing ballads sung, they may not need to hear a full version of the story — they can fill out the singer's performance from their own prior knowledge. It is open to the singer, too, in direct contact with an audience to give prose additions to the story and to enter into discussion about the motivation of the characters. In these conditions the ballad is not an isolated entity. Then again, the ballad as performed to be taken down by a collector is in a very special context of its own. Finally, with or without having passed through such an intermediary stage, the ballad may be recontextualised in the course of its history in a drawing-room setting with piano accompaniment or in a folk-club setting, perhaps sung to the guitar.

One broader, less immediate, context is the national one. The early Scottish collectors were driven by a conscious desire to preserve an element of their national heritage and their publications proudly presented their discoveries. The ballads had been Scottish in the sense that they had been collected in Scotland, but they soon became something that provided extra nourishment for Scottish identity.

How Scottish *are* these ballads? Ballads were transmitted

freely among the various English-speaking parts of the British Isles and have been carried overseas by emigrants and other travellers to start up fresh lives in their new settings.[10] It is notable, however, that over a period of several centuries Scotland seems both to have initiated ballads and to have provided an especially hospitable environment for those that came from elsewhere.[11]

Some of the ballads represented here have strong links with England — for example, 'Young Bicham' where the hero says 'London city is my own', and 'The Jew's Daughter' which concerns Hugh of Lincoln — but they were sung widely in Scotland and it may be noted that the place-name 'Lincoln' has been eroded away in a number of Scottish versions so that the ballad concerned is no longer identifiably English. Names are among the most easily altered features of ballads and changes are often made to bring in locations more familiar to the singers.

Ballads have come to Scotland from further afield than England. A number of them are sung in other languages throughout Europe and here an actual process of translation has been involved as well as a relocalisation of the narrative. The narrative of 'The Douglas Tragedy', for example, is found widely in Scandinavian ballad tradition and ballads corresponding to 'Lord Ronald' occur in Italian, Dutch, Swedish, Hungarian and Slavic versions.

One feature that has been remarked upon in Scottish ballads is that they have an especially strong element of the supernatural, sometimes experienced directly as meetings with supernatural beings, and sometimes sensed through dreams and prognostications. A striking comparison can be made in the case of 'The Daemon Lover', where the earliest English version is a broadside headed (not very succinctly) *A Warning for Married Women, being an example of Mrs Jane Reynolds (a West-country woman), born near Plymouth, who, having plighted her troth to a Seaman, was afterwards married to a Carpenter, and at last carried away by a Spirit, the manner how shall presently be recited.* There is an element of the supernatural in both versions, but the 'spirit' of the English version is replaced by the much more powerful figure of the devil himself in the Scottish form, and the English broadside has no equivalent to the devil's words (verses 13-14):

'O what hills are yon, yon pleasant hills,
    That the sun shines sweetly on?'
'O yon are the hills of heaven,' he said,
    'Where you will never win.'

'O whaten a mountain is yon,' she said,
    'All so dreary wi frost and snow?'
'O yon is the mountain of hell,' he cried,
    'Where you and I will go.'

This, with its stark alternatives of good and evil, can be said to be a Christian formulation which may be found in other ballads too, such as 'The Maid of Coldingham'. But we also have elements that come from a pre-Christian world-view, as when we glimpse an otherworld that is neither heaven *nor* hell in 'Thomas the Rhymer' (verses 11-13):

'O see ye not yon narrow road,
    So thick beset with thorns and briers?
That is the path of righteousness,
    Tho after it but few enquires.

'And see not ye that braid braid road,
    That lies across that lily leven?
That is the path of wickedness,
    Tho some call it the road to heaven.

'And see not ye that bonny road,
    That winds about the fernie brae?
That is the road to fair Elfland,
    Where thou and I this night maun gae.

The magic that enters the ballads on Scottish soil, however, is not purely a matter of the supernatural, as everyone who feels this magic knows. It is the language itself that has an inimitable magic, which I think may lie partly in the balance between what is said and what is not said — if what is not said may be claimed to be part of language. These songs are narratives, but the proportion of intense climax to story is high. One can trace a tendency in ballads to move from the narrative to the lyric as singers focus on the high emotional points of a story, as in this fragmentary version of 'The Baron of Brackley' (cf. the version in this edition):

> 'Oh come ye by Braikley, oh come ye by there?
> Saw ye a fair lady, she was kaimin her hair?'
> 'She was dancin an singin, she was dancin wi joy
> For young Jamie Braikley, the flooer o them a.'

> 'Get up Betsy Gordon, and gie me yer gun
> For if I gang oot, I will never come in.'
> Oh first he killed one and then he's killed twa
> And he killed Jamie Braikley, the flooer o them a.

> 'Oh cam ye by Braikley, oh cam ye by there?
> Saw ye a fair lady, she was kaimin her hair?'
> 'She was dancin an singin, an dancin wi joy
> For young Jamie Braikley, the flooer o them a.'[12]

Fragments like this can have great power, especially when sung, but they cannot stand alone without commentary. What we seem to have in the finest ballads is the result of a movement towards lyric which has dropped the prosaic features of the narrative, while still retaining just enough to carry the story, sometimes by implication only.

The moulding of the ballads has been partly a matter of the versions known traditionally to the singer and partly a matter of that singer's own practice, but we also have to take account of a third component to do with our cultural expectations concerning the singer's role.

In some cultures a singer is called upon to transmit a song precisely and word for word as it is received and this may be especially true of songs that are regarded as holy, or where the original author's words are sacrosanct. At the other extreme, the singer's creativity is valued and he or she is expected to produce something completely fresh in detail while still following the main lines of the narrative. This is the case with the epics sung in the Balkans and, since the publication of Albert Lord's *Singer of Tales* in 1960,[13] all potentially oral canons have been subjected to scrutiny to see how far they use formulas in the same way that the Yugoslav epic singers did, to create each song afresh at the time of singing. David Buchan took this up in relation to Scottish ballads[14] and went beyond the evidence in claiming that, whereas all other Scottish ballads are affected by the context of literacy, the ballads as sung by one of our earliest fine ballad singers, Anna Gordon (Mrs Brown), were the result of a process of knowing a storyline and re-clothing it with words at each performance. Closer attention to repertoires is increasing our understanding of the singers' roles,[15] and it seems more fruitful to posit a continuum among Scottish ballad singers of various personalities at various periods, rather than propose a sharp break in their mode of creation with Anna Gordon and her lost predecessors on the one side, and all other known singers on the other.[16]

Buchan's pioneering work has, however, opened up ballad studies to a keen awareness of oral process. Memory has always been a factor, but what is remembered may vary, for it can be a mix of storylines, structures, formulas and verbal strings. Embedded structures can be aesthetically rewarding and can *also* be aids to oral composition, as for example in the cases of the binary, trinary and framing patterns highlighted by Buchan.[17] One common type of pairing is the question and its mirroring answer as in verses 2 and 3 of 'Lord Thomas and Fair Annie':

> 'But wha will bake my bridal bread,
>> Or brew my bridal ale?
> And wha will welcome my brisk bride,
>> That I bring oer the dale?'

'It's I will bake your bridal bread,
  And brew your bridal ale,
And I will welcome your brisk bride,
  That you bring oer the dale.'

Pairing and triadic patterns may occur internally within a
verse, as in the triad in verse 29 of 'Wee Messgrove':

'Oh weel I like his cheeks,' she said,
  'And weel I like his chin;
And better I like his fair bodie
  Than a' your kith and kin.'

A triadic structure applied over three verses may be illustrated
by verses 3-5 of 'Bob Norris':

Gae tack to her this pair o gluves
  Thay'r o the sillar grey
An tell her to cum to the merrie grein wud
  An speik to Bob Norrise

Gae tack to her this gay gowd ring
  Its aw gowd but the stane
An tell her to cum to the merrie grein wud
  An ask the leive of nane

Gae tack to her this gay manteil
  It's aw silk but the sleive
An tell her to cum to the merrie grein wud
  An ask nae bauld baron's leive

Framing or ring patterns occur where parts of a ballad distant
from each other are tied together by similarities or contrasts
in words and ideas, and by their positions enclosing a
distinctive section of text. These devices, too, like the binary
and trinary structures, play an important role in the production
of the ballads.

Another aspect of construction that is simultaneously an
aid to singers and a part of what gives the ballads their
distinctive feel is the use of formulas, as when someone about
to set out on a journey signals this by calling for a horse to be
saddled in lines like those in verse 9 of 'Johny Faa, the Gypsy

Laddie' and verse 11 of 'Bog o' Gight':

> 'Gae saddle to me the black, black steed,
>   Gae saddle and make him ready'

> Go saddle to me the black horse she cried
>   The brown never rode so boldly

As Flemming Andersen has noted,[18] these formulas convey meaning at the level of deep structure, so that even when the surface details differ the same fundamental meaning comes through. The same notion of deep structure goes a long way towards explaining the impact of what has been called 'incremental repetition', as in the closing verses of 'Sir Patrick Spens'. It is not so much that the second verse gives added information, as that the changing details are substituted for each other so that we cannot rest in them alone but feel the deep structure that is common to the two images, in this case a sense of unending grief.

> O lang, lang may the ladyes sit,
>   Wi their fans into their hand,
> Before they see Sir Patrick Spens
>   Come sailing to the strand.

> And lang, lang may the maidens sit,
>   Wi their goud kaims in their hair,
> A' waiting for their ain dear loves,
>   For them they'll see na mair.

The people from whom we received these ballads engaged confidently with the great themes of love and death. They would often have thought that their stories were true (although in many cases this is not so), and they would have had a direct personal sympathy for the characters. But literal truth is not the only truth, and no singer can have failed to experience the *emotional* truths encapsulated in these ballad narratives. That inner reality is as strong for us today as it was for the singers of earlier centuries, even if we do see the ballad world from a rather different perspective. It is a world where kings and shepherds, ladies and dairy maids are juxtaposed and where the everyday is mingled with various kinds of 'otherness', including what was already 'long ago' for the singers. Now their present, too, has become the past and, since the boundaries of the everyday have shifted so violently since the time of horseback travel, we experience a ballad world which has a much greater degree of otherness than it once had. When the young woman in 'The Laird o' Drum' speaks of milking 'the cow or the ewe / Wi the cogie on [her] knee', this action was in the everyday realm, whereas for us it is part of a lost rural heritage which interests and intrigues us precisely because it no longer belongs to everyday life.

Of course, the supernatural that marks so many of these songs was and remains strongly 'other', but the ballads exert an equal fascination whether they are 'everyday' or 'long ago', 'supernatural' or 'this-worldly'. Whatever differences of interpretation they may have undergone throughout their long and varied history, the force of their tales and the force of their telling are as alive today as they ever were.

Emily Lyle

NOTES

1. On Burns and his oral context, see Mary Ellen Brown, *Burns and Tradition* (London 1984).

2. For general background, see Ruth Finnegan, *Oral Poetry: its Nature, Significance and Social Context* (Cambridge 1977; 2nd edn Bloomington, Indiana, 1991), and for bibliographic guides to ballad scholarship, see David C. Fowler, 'XV. Ballads' in *A Manual of the Writings in Middle English 1050-1500*, gen. eds. J. Burke Severs and Albert E. Hartung (New Haven, Connecticut, 1980), 6.1753-1808, 2019-70, and W. Edson Richmond, *Ballad Scholarship: An Annotated Bibliography* (New York and London 1989).

3. E. B. Lyle, 'The Relationship between "Thomas the Rhymer" and "Thomas of Erceldoune"', *Leeds Studies in English* 4, 23-30.

4. British Library, MS Cotton Vespasian A.25, No 67, fol. 187.

5. For discussion of how best to cope with the gaps in our knowledge, see Emily Lyle, 'Parity of Ignorance: Child's Judgment on "Sir Colin" and the Scottish Verdict "Not Proven"' in *The Ballad and Oral Literature* ed. Joseph Harris (Cambridge, Mass., 1991), pp. 109-15.

6. Marion Stewart, 'A Recently-Discovered Manuscript: "ane taill of Sir colling ye knyt"', *Scottish Studies* 16 (1972), 23-39, lines 56-71. Letter forms have been modernised; 'allreche', 'compeir' and 'wad' can be glossed as 'elven', 'appear' and 'token'.

7. Cf. Bertrand Harris Bronson, *The Ballad as Song* (Berkeley and Los Angeles 1969), Hamish Henderson,

Alias MacAlias: Writings on Songs, Folk and Literature, (Edinburgh 1992), Ailie Munro, *The Folk Music Revival in Scotland* (London 1984, 2nd edn Aberdeen forthcoming) and James Porter, *The Traditional Music of Britain and Ireland: A Research and Information Guide* (New York and London 1989).

8. Recordings from the archive of the School of Scottish Studies, with accompanying booklet, are available in *The Muckle Sangs* (Scottish Tradition 5), CDTRAX 9005 and CTRAX 9005. A *Scottish Ballads* cassette is being issued as a companion to the present edition.

9. Cf. Richard Bauman and Charles L. Briggs, 'Poetics and Performance as Critical Perspectives on Language and Social Life,' *Annual Review of Anthropology* 19 (1990), 59-88.

10. See, for example, the annotated bibliography of North American ballad tradition, *The British Traditional Ballad in North America*, ed. Tristram P. Coffin and Roger Renwick (Austin, Texas, 1977).

11. This does not apply to Gaelic-speaking Scotland. On the slender tradition of ballads in Irish and Scottish Gaelic, see Hugh Shields, *Narrative Songs in Ireland: Lays, Ballads, Come-All-Yes and Other Songs* (Dublin 1993), pp. 55-6, 66-9.

12. Recording from Lucy Stewart by Kenneth Goldstein, Fetterangus, April 1960.

13. Albert B. Lord, *The Singer of Tales* (Cambridge, Mass., 1960, reprint 1981) and John Miles Foley, *Oral-Formulaic Theory and Research: An Introduction and Annotated Bibliography* (New York and London 1985).

14. David Buchan, *The Ballad and the Folk* (London 1972, reprint Edinburgh 1994).

15. See, for example, the book-length studies of the repertoires of Agnes Lyle and Jeannie Robertson: William Bernard McCarthy, *The Ballad Matrix: Personality, Milieu, and the Oral Tradition* (Bloomington and Indianapolis 1990) and Herschel Gower and James Porter, *Jeannie Robertson and her Songs* (Knoxville, Tennessee, forthcoming).

16. Cf. Flemming G. Andersen and Thomas Pettitt, 'Mrs Brown of Falkland: A Singer of Tales?' *Journal of American Folklore* 92 (1979), 1-24, and Hamish Henderson, 'The Ballad, the Folk and the Oral Tradition' in *The People's Past*, ed. Edward J. Cowan (Edinburgh 1980, reprint 1991).

17. David Buchan, *The Ballad and the Folk* (London 1972), pp. 87-104.

18. Flemming G. Andersen, *Commonplace and Creativity: The Role of Formulaic Diction in Anglo-Scottish Traditional Balladry* (Odense 1985), pp. 33-7.

Note on Language and Sources

Glosses are given in this edition where the wording might present difficulty, but it has not been thought necessary to gloss the following commonly found Scots words:

aboon, abune *above*
ae *one, only*
ay, aye *always, continually*
bairn *child*
bonnie *pretty, attractive, beautiful*
bower *chamber, room*
braw *fine, finely dressed*
bree, brie *brow*
ee, een *eye, eyes*
frae *from*
gae *gave*
gaed, ged *went*
gang *go*
gar *cause, make*
gear *property*
gie, gi *give*
gin *if*
gowd *gold*
grat *wept, cried*
greet *weep, cry*
hae *have*
intill *into, in*
ken *know*
kirk *church*

lad *boy, young man*
laird *landowner*
lass, lassie *girl*
light, light down *alight, dismount*
maun *must*
mirk *dark*
muckle, mickle, meikle *great, much*
ohon *exclamation of sorrow*
pin *door fastening*
ring *part of door handle*
shoon, sheen *shoes*
sic *such*
syne *then*
(the) tane, tae *the one*
till *to*
tirl *rattle*
(the) tother, tither *the other*
wan *pale, dull, lustreless*
(I) wat, wot *I know, indeed*
wee *little*
yate, yett *gate*

The sources of the texts given here are listed in the notes and the singers are identified wherever possible. All the ballads are what are called 'Child ballads' since they are included in *The English and Scottish Popular Ballads* (Boston 1882-98) compiled by the American scholar Francis James Child, and many of the texts are drawn from his edition. This source has been supplemented by the addition of versions that were not located by Child or that are more recent than his time. When we know the actual tune that went with the version of words given here, a reference to it is included in the notes. Other tune versions can readily be found in *The Traditional Tunes of the Child Ballads* edited by Bertrand H. Bronson in four volumes (Princeton, N.J., 1959-72), or the one-volume abbreviated form of it called *The Singing Tradition of Child's Popular Ballads* (Princeton, N.J., 1976).

SCOTTISH BALLADS

I

The Battle of Otterburn

1 It fell about the Lammas tide,
  When the muir-men win their hay,
The doughty Douglas bound him to ride
  Into England, to drive a prey.

2 He chose the Gordons and the Graemes.
  With them the Lindesays, light and gay;
But the Jardines wald not with him ride,
  And they rue it to this day.

3 And he has burnd the dales of Tyne,
  And part of Bambrough shire,
And three good towers on Reidswire fells,
  He left them all on fire.

4 And he marchd up to Newcastle,
  And rode it round about:
'O wha's the lord of this castle?
  Or wha's the lady o't?'

5 But up spake proud Lord Percy then,
  And O but he spake hie!
I am the lord of this castle,
  My wife's the lady gay.

6 'If thou'rt the lord of this castle,
  Sae weel it pleases me,
For, ere I cross the Border fells,
  The tane of us shall die.'

1 Lammas *1st of August* · muir-men win *moor-men
gather in* · doughty *formidable* · bound him *got
ready* · drive a prey *drive off cattle as booty*
5 hie *arrogantly*
6 fells *hills*

7 He took a lang spear in his hand,
  Shod with the metal free,
And for to meet the Douglas there
  He rode right furiouslie.

8 But O how pale his lady lookd,
  Frae aff the castle-wa,
When down before the Scottish spear
  She saw proud Percy fa.

9 'Had we twa been upon the green,
  And never an eye to see,
I wad hae had you, flesh and fell;
  But your sword sall gae wi me.'

10 'But gae ye up to Otterbourne,
  And, wait there dayis three,
And, if I come not ere three dayis end,
  A fause knight ca ye me.'

11 'The Otterbourne 's a bonnie burn;
  'T is pleasant there to be;
But there is nought at Otterbourne
  To feed my men and me.

12 'The deer rins wild on hill and dale,
  The birds fly wild from tree to tree;
But there is neither bread nor kale
  To fend my men and me.

13 'Yet I will stay at Otterbourne,
  Where you shall welcome be;
And, if ye come not at three dayis end,
  A fause lord I'll ca thee.'

7 free *good*
9 fell *skin*
12 kale *a kind of cabbage* · fend *provision*

14 'Thither will I come,' proud Percy said,
     'By the might of Our Ladye;'
   'There will I bide thee,' said the Douglas,
     'My troth I plight to thee.'

15 They lighted high on Otterbourne,
     Upon the bent sae brown;
   They lighted high on Otterbourne,
     And threw their pallions down.

16 And he that had a bonnie boy,
     Sent out his horse to grass;
   And he that had not a bonnie boy,
     His ain servant he was.

17 But up then spake a little page,
     Before the peep of dawn:
   'O waken ye, waken ye, my good lord,
     For Percy's hard at hand.'

18 'Ye lie, ye lie, ye liar loud!
     Sae loud I hear ye lie:
   For Percy had not men yestreen
     To dight my men and me.

19 'But I have dreamd a dreary dream,
     Beyond the Isle of Sky;
   I saw a dead man win a fight,
     And I think that man was I.'

20 He belted on his guid braid sword,
     And to the field he ran,
   But he forgot the helmet good,
     That should have kept his brain.

15 bent *coarse grass* · pallions *pavilions*
17 hard at hand *near by*
18 dight *cope with*
19 dreary *foreboding*
20 kept *protected*

21 When Percy wi the Douglas met,
     I wat he was fu fain;
   They swakked their swords, till sair they swat,
     And the blood ran down like rain.

22 But Percy with his good broad sword,
     That could so sharply wound,
   Has wounded Douglas on the brow,
     Till he fell to the ground.

23 Then he calld on his little foot-page,
     And said, Run speedilie,
   And fetch my ain dear sister's son,
     Sir Hugh Montgomery.

24 'My nephew good,' the Douglas said,
     'What recks the death of ane!
   Last night I dreamd a dreary dream,
     And I ken the day's thy ain.

25 'My wound is deep; I fain would sleep;
     Take thou the vanguard of the three,
   And hide me by the braken-bush,
     That grows on yonder lilye lee.

26 'O bury me by the braken-bush,
     Beneath the blooming brier;
   Let never living mortal ken
     That ere a kindly Scot lies here.'

27 He lifted up that noble lord,
     Wi the saut tear in his ee;
   He hid him in the braken-bush,
     That his merrie men might not see.

21 fain *eager* · swakked *smote* · swat *sweated*
24 recks *matters*
25 fain would sleep *would like to sleep*
25 braken-bush *clump of fern* · lilye lee *fair grass land*

28　The moon was clear, the day drew near,
　　　　The spears in flinders flew,
　　But mony a gallant Englishman
　　　　Ere day the Scotsmen slew.

29　The Gordons good, in English blood
　　　　They steepd their hose and shoon;
　　The Lindsays flew like fire about,
　　　　Till all the fray was done.

30　The Percy and Montgomery met,
　　　　That either of other were fain;
　　They swapped swords, and they twa swat,
　　　　And aye the blood ran down between.

31　'Now yield thee, yield thee, Percy,' he said,
　　　　'Or else I vow I'll lay thee low!'
　　'To whom must I yield,' quoth Earl Percy,
　　　　'Now that I see it must be so?'

32　'Thou shalt not yield to lord nor loun,
　　　　Nor yet shalt thou yield to me;
　　But yield thee to the braken-bush,
　　　　That grows upon yon lilye lee.'

33　'I will not yield to a braken-bush,
　　　　Nor yet will I yield to a brier;
　　But I would yield to Earl Douglas,
　　　　Or Sir Hugh the Montgomery, if he were here.'

34　As soon as he knew it was Montgomery,
　　　　He struck his sword's point in the gronde;
　　The Montgomery was a courteous knight,
　　　　And quickly took him by the honde.

28 flinders *splinters*
30 fain *glad* · swapped *smote*
32 loun *man of low rank*

35 This deed was done at the Otterbourne,
About the breaking of the day;
Earl Douglas was buried at the braken-bush,
And the Percy led captive away.

2

Kinmont Willie

1 O have ye na heard o the fause Sakelde?
O have ye na heard o the keen Lord Scroop?
How they hae taen bauld Kinmont Willie,
On Hairibee to hang him up?

2 Had Willie had but twenty men,
But twenty men as stout as he,
Fause Sakelde had never the Kinmont taen,
Wi eight score in his companie.

3 They band his legs beneath the steed,
They tied his hands behind his back;
They guarded him, fivesome on each side,
And they brought him ower the Liddel-rack.

4 They led him thro the Liddel-rack,
And also thro the Carlisle sands;
They brought him to Carlisle castell,
To be at my Lord Scroope's commands.

5 'My hands are tied, but my tongue is free,
And whae will dare this deed avow?
Or answer by the border law?
Or answer to the bauld Buccleuch?'

1 keen *bold*
3 Liddel-rack *Liddel ford*
5 avow *confess*

6 'Now haud thy tongue, thou rank reiver!
     There's never a Scot shall set ye free;
 Before ye cross my castle-yate,
     I trow ye shall take farewell o me.'

7 'Fear na ye that, my lord,' quo Willie;
     'By the faith o my bodie, Lord Scroop,' he said,
 'I never yet lodged in a hostelrie
     But I paid my lawing before I gaed.'

8 Now word is gane to the bauld Keeper,
     In Branksome Ha where that he lay,
 That Lord Scroope has taen the Kinmont Willie,
     Between the hours of night and day.

9 He has taen the table wi his hand,
     He garrd the red wine spring on hie;
 'Now Christ's curse on my head,' he said,
     'But avenged of Lord Scroop I'll be!

10 'O is my basnet a widow's curch?
     Or my lance a wand of the willow-tree?
 Or my arm a ladye's lilye hand?
     That an English lord should lightly me.

11 'And have they taen him Kinmont Willie,
     Against the truce of Border tide,
 And forgotten that the bauld Bacleuch
     Is keeper here on the Scottish side?

12 'And have they een taen him Kinmont Willie,
     Withouten either dread or fear,
 And forgotten that the bauld Bacleuch
     Can back a steed, or shake a spear?

6 rank *violent* · reiver *robber* · castle-yate *castle gate* ·
I trow *assuredly*
7 lawing *reckoning, bill*
10 basnet *skull-cap helmet* · curch *head-covering* ·
lightly *make light of, treat with disrespect*

13 'O were there war between the lands,
        As well I wot that there is none,
    I would slight Carlisle castell high,
        Tho it were builded of marble-stone.

14 'I would set that castell in a low,
        And sloken it with English blood;
    There's nevir a man in Cumberland
        Should ken where Carlisle castell stood.

15 'But since nae war's between the lands,
        And there is peace, and peace should be,
    I'll neither harm English lad or lass,
        And yet the Kinmont freed shall be!'

16 He has calld him forty marchmen bauld,
        I trow they were of his ain name,
    Except Sir Gilbert Elliot, calld
        The Laird of Stobs, I mean the same.

17 He has calld him forty marchmen bauld,
        Were kinsmen to the bauld Buccleuch,
    With spur on heel, and splent on spauld,
        And gleuves of green, and feathers blue.

18 There were five and five before them a',
        Wi hunting-horns and bugles bright;
    And five and five came wi Buccleuch,
        Like Warden's men, arrayed for fight.

19 And five and five like a mason-gang,
        That carried the ladders lang and hie;
    And five and five like broken men;
        And so they reached the Woodhouselee.

13 slight *demolish*
14 low *blaze* · sloken *quench*
16 marchmen *Borderers*
17 splent *plate armour* · spauld *shoulder* · gleuves *gloves*
19 broken men *outlaws*

20 And as we crossd the Bateable Land,
         When to the English side we held,
     The first o men that we met wi,
         Whae sould it be but fause Sakelde!

21 'Where be ye gaun, ye hunters keen?'
         Quo fause Sakelde; 'come tell to me!'
     'We go to hunt an English stag,
         Has trespassed on the Scots countrie.'

22 'Where be ye gaun, ye marshal-men?'
         Quo fause Sakelde; 'come tell me true!'
     'We go to catch a rank reiver,
         Has broken faith wi the bauld Buccleuch.'

23 'Where are ye gaun, ye mason-lads,
         Wi a' your ladders lang and hie?'
     'We gang to herry a corbie's nest,
         That wons not far frae Woodhouselee.'

24 'Where be ye gaun, ye broken men?'
         Quo fause Sakelde; 'come tell to me!'
     Now Dickie of Dryhope led that band,
         And the nevir a word o lear had he.

25 'Why trespass ye on the English side?
         Row-footed outlaws, stand!' quo he;
     The neer a word had Dickie to say,
         Sae he thrust the lance thro his fause bodie.

26 Then on we held for Carlisle toun,
         And at Staneshaw-bank the Eden we crossd;
     The water was great, and meikle of spait,
         But the nevir a horse nor man we lost.

20 Bateable *Debatable*
23 herry *rob* · corbie's *raven's, crow's* · wons *dwells*
24 lear *learning* · 25 row-footed *rough-shod, wearing*
shoes of undressed hide with the hair still on
26 meikle of spait *in full flood*

27 And when we reachd the Staneshaw-bank,
    The wind was rising loud and hie;
And there the laird garrd leave our steeds,
    For fear that they should stamp and nie.

28 And when we left the Staneshaw-bank,
    The wind began full loud to blaw;
But 't was wind and weet, and fire and sleet,
    When we came beneath the castel-wa.

29 We crept on knees, and held our breath,
    Till we placed the ladders against the wa;
And saw ready was Buccleuch himsell
    To mount the first before us a'.

30 He has taen the watchman by the throat,
    He flung him down upon the lead:
'Had there not been peace between our lands,
    Upon the other side thou hadst gaed.

31 'Now sound out, trumpets!' quo Buccleuch;
    'Let's waken Lord Scroope right merrilie!'
Then loud the Warden's trumpets blew
    'O whae dare meddle wi me?'

32 Then speedilie to wark we gaed,
    And raised the slogan ane and a',
And cut a hole thro a sheet of lead,
    And so we wan to the castel-ha.

33 They thought King James and a' his men
    Had won the house wi bow and speir;
It was but twenty Scots and ten
    That put a thousand in sic a stear!

28 weet *rain*
30 lead *roof*
32 slogan *war-cry* · wan *reached*
33 won *captured* · stear *commotion*

34 Wi coulters and wi forehammers,
     We garrd the bars bang merrilie,
  Untill we came to the inner prison,
     Where Willie o Kinmont he did lie.

35 And when we cam to the lower prison,
     Where Willie o Kinmont he did lie,
  'O sleep ye, wake ye, Kinmont Willie,
     Upon the morn that thou's to die?'

36 'O I sleep saft, and I wake aft,
     It's lang since sleeping was fleyd frae me;
  Gie my service back to my wyfe and bairns,
     And a' gude fellows that speer for me.'

37 Then Red Rowan has hente him up,
     The starkest men in Teviotdale:
  'Abide, abide now, Red Rowan,
     Till of my Lord Scroope I take farewell.

38 'Farewell, farewell, my gude Lord Scroope!
     My gude Lord Scroope, farewell!' he cried;
  'I'll pay you for my lodging-maill
     When first we meet on the border-side.'

39 Then shoulder high, with shout and cry,
     We bore him down the ladder lang;
  At every stride Red Rowan made,
     I wot the Kinmont's airns playd clang.

34 forehammers *sledge-hammers*
36 fleyd frae me *driven out of me by fear* · speer *ask*
37 hente *picked* · starkest *strongest* · abide *wait*
38 lodging-maill *rent for lodging*
39 airns playd clang *irons clanged together*

40 'O mony a time,' quo Kinmont Willie,
    'I have ridden horse baith wild and wood;
But a rougher beast than Red Rowan
    I ween my legs have neer bestrode.

41 'And mony a time,' quo Kinmont Willie,
    'I've pricked a horse out oure the furs;
But since the day I backed a steed
    I nevir wore sic cumbrous spurs.'

42 We scarce had won the Staneshaw-bank,
    When a' the Carlisle bells were rung,
And a thousand men, in horse and foot,
    Cam wi the keen Lord Scroope along.

43 Buccleuch has turned to Eden Water,
    Even where it flowd frae bank to brim,
And he has plunged in wi a' his band,
    And safely swam them thro the stream.

44 He turned him on the other side,
    And at Lord Scroope his glove flung he:
'If ye like na my visit in merry England,
    In fair Scotland come visit me!'

45 All sore astonished stood Lord Scroope,
    He stood as still as rock of stane;
He scarcely dared to trew his eyes
    When thro the water they had gane.

46 'He is either himsell a devil frae hell,
    Or else his mother a witch maun be;
I wad na have ridden that wan water
    For a' the gowd in Christentie.'

40 wood *crazy* · ween *think*
41 pricked *spurred* · out oure the furs *away over the furrows* · backed *got on a horse's back* · cumbrous *cumbersome*
45 trew *believe*

3

Johnie Armstrang

1 Sum speiks of lords, sum speiks of lairds,
····And siclyke men of hie degrie;
··Of a gentleman I sing a sang,
····Sumtyme calld Laird of Gilnockie.

2 The king he wrytes a luving letter,
····With his ain hand sae tenderly:
··And he hath sent it to Johny Armstrang,
····To cum and speik with him speidily.

3 The Eliots and Armstrangs did convene,
····They were a gallant company:
··'We'ill ryde and meit our lawful king,
····And bring him safe to Gilnockie.

4 'Make kinnen and capon ready, then,
····And venison in great plenty;
··We'ill welcome hame our royal king;
····I hope he'ill dyne at Gilnockie!'

5 They ran their horse on the Langum howm,
····And brake their speirs with mekle main;
··The ladys lukit frae their loft-windows,
····'God bring our men weil back again!'

6 When Johny came before the king,
····With all his men sae brave to see,
··The king he movit his bonnet to him;
····He weind he was a king as well as he.

1 siclyke men *men like that* · degrie *rank* ·
sumtyme *at one time*
4 kinnen *rabbit* · capon *cock*
5 howm *level ground by river* · main *force*
6 movit *took off* · weind *thought*

7 'May I find grace, my sovereign liege,
    Grace for my loyal men and me?
For my name it is Johny Armstrang,
    And subject of yours, my liege,' said he.

8 'Away, away, thou traytor strang!
    Out of my sicht thou mayst sune be!
I grantit nevir a traytors lyfe,
    And now I'll not begin with thee.'

9 'Grant me my lyfe, my liege, my king,
    And a bony gift I will give to thee;
Full four-and twenty milk-whyt steids,
    Were a' foald in a yeir to me.

10 'I'll gie thee all these milk-whyt steids,
    That prance and nicher at a speir,
With as mekle gude Inglis gilt
    As four of their braid backs dow beir.'

11 'Away, away, thou traytor strang!
    Out o' my sicht thou mayst sune be!
I grantit nevir a traytors lyfe,
    And now I'll not begin with thee.'

12 'Grant me my lyfe, my liege, my king,
    And a bony gift I'll gie to thee;
Gude four-and-twenty ganging mills,
    That gang throw a' the yeir to me.

13 'These four-and-twenty mills complete
    Sall gang for thee throw all the yeir,
And as mekle of gude reid wheit
    As all their happers dow to bear.'

8 strang *violent*
10 nicher *neigh* · Inglis gilt *English gold*
12 ganging *working*
13 happers dow to bear *hoppers can contain*

14 'Away, away, thou traytor strang!
        Out of my sicht thou mayst sune be!
    I grantit nevir a traytors lyfe,
        And now I'll not begin with thee.'

15 'Grant me my lyfe, my liege, my king,
        And a great gift I'll gie to thee;
    Bauld four-and-twenty sisters sons,
        Sall for the fecht, tho all sould flee.'

16 'Away, away, thou traytor strang!
        Out of my sicht thou mayst sune be!
    I grantit nevir a traytors lyfe,
        And now I'll not begin with thee.'

17 'Grant me my lyfe, my liege, my king,
        And a brave gift I'll gie to thee;
    All betwene heir and Newcastle town
        Sall pay thair yeirly rent to thee.'

18 'Away, away, thou traytor strang!
        Out of my sicht thou mayst sune be!
    I grantit nevir a traytors lyfe,
        And now I'll not begin with thee.'

19 'Ye lied, ye lied, now, king,' he says,
        'Althocht a king and prince ye be,
    For I luid naithing in all my lyfe,
        I dare well say it, but honesty;

20 'But a fat horse, and a fair woman,
        Twa bony dogs to kill a deir:
    But Ingland suld haif found me meil and malt,
        Gif I had livd this hundred yeir!

19 luid *loved*
20 fat *well-fed* · found me *supplied me with*

[41]

21 'Scho suld haif found me meil and malt,
   And beif and mutton in all plentie;
But neir a Scots wyfe could haif said
   That eir I skaithd her a pure flie.

22 'To seik het water beneth cauld yce,
   Surely it is a great folie;
I haif asked grace at a graceless face,
   But there is nane for my men and me.

23 'But had I kend, or I came frae hame,
   How thou unkynd wadst bene to me,
I wad haif kept the border-syde,
   In spyte of all thy force and thee.

24 'Wist Englands king that I was tane,
   O gin a blyth man wald he be!
For anes I slew his sisters son,
   And on his breist-bane brak a tree.'

25 John wore a girdle about his middle,
   Imbroiderd owre with burning gold,
Bespangled with the same mettle,
   Maist beautifull was to behold.

26 Ther hang nine targats at Johnys hat,
   And ilk an worth three hundred pound:
'What wants that knave that a king suld haif,
   But the sword of honour and the crown!

21 wyfe *woman* · skaithd her a pure flie *did her a
whit of harm*
23 or *before* · unkynd *unnaturally severe* · kept
defended
24 wist *knew* · tane *taken, captured* · anes *once* ·
tree *spear*
26 targats *shield-shaped ornaments* · ilk an *each one*

27 'O whair gat thou these targats, Johnie,
        That blink sae brawly abune thy brie?'
    'I gat them in the field fechting,
        Wher, cruel king, thou durst not be.

28 'Had I my horse, and my harness gude,
        And ryding as I wont to be,
    It sould haif bene tald this hundred yeir
        The meiting of my king and me.

29 'God be withee, Kirsty, my brither,
        Lang live thou Laird of Mangertoun!
    Lang mayst thou live on the border-syde
        Or thou se thy brither ryde up and doun.

30 'And God be withee, Kirsty, my son,
        Whair thou sits on thy nurses knee!
    But and thou live this hundred yeir,
        Thy fathers better thoult never be.

31 'Farweil, my bonny Gilnock-Hall,
        Whair on Esk-syde thou standest stout!
    Gif I had lived but seven yeirs mair,
        I wald haif gilt thee round about.'

32 John murdred was at Carlinrigg,
        And all his galant companie:
    But Scotlands heart was never sae wae,
        To see sae mony brave men die.

33 Because they savd their country deir
        Frae Englishmen; nane were sae bauld,
    Whyle Johnie livd on the border-syde,
        Nane of them durst cum neir his hald.

27 blink *shine* · brawly *splendidly*
30 but and *but if*
32 wae *sad*
33 hald *stronghold*

4

The Battle o' Harlaw

1 As I cam in the Geerie lan's,
    And in by Netherha',
I saw sixty thoosan redcoats
    A' marchin to Harlaw.
        Wi' my derry dey, dumpty dow,
        A daddle um a dee.

2 As I cam on, and farther on,
    Till I cam to Balquhain,
Fa was there but James the Rose,
    An wi' him was John Graeme?

3 O, did ye fae the Heilans come,
    Or did ye come that wye?
Or did ye see Macdonal's men,
    As they cam fae the Skye?

4 O yes, me fae the Hielans cam,
    And me cam a' the wye,
And I did see Macdonal's men,
    As they cam fae the Skye?

5 O, was ye very near them,
    Did you their number see?
Or could ye tell, John Hielanman,
    What might their number be?

6 O yes, me was near them,
    And me their number saw,
There was ninety thoosen Hielanmen
    A marchin to Harlaw.

2 fa *who*

7 If that be true, says James the Rose,
       We'll sheath our swords wi' speed,
   And then call in our merry young men,
       And lightly mount our steed.

8 O no, O no, said John the Graeme,
       O no, that must not be;
   The Rose's clans was never cowards
       What man can do we'll try.

9 So they rode on, and farther on,
       Till they cam to Harlaw;
   They both fell fast on every side,
       Such fun you never saw.

10 The Hielanmen they were behind,
        The redcoats before,
    And they beat back the redcoats
        Two acres' breadth and more.

11 Brave Forbes to his brother said,
        O brother, don't you see
    How they beat our men on every side,
        And we'll be forced to flee?

12 O no, O no, my brother dear,
        O no, that must not be;
    You'll take your broadsword in your hand,
        Go in the ranks wi' me.

13 O no, O no, my brother,
        Their clans they are too strong,
    Don't you see that cursed Hielanmen
        Wi' heavy swords and long?

14 Brave Forbes to his merry men called,
        You'll take your breath a while,
    Till I do put my servant
        To bring my coat o' mail.

15 His servant to Drumminor rode,
    His horse he didna fail;
    In two oors and a quarter
    He brought his coat o' mail.

16 Noo back to back this twa fierce lords
    They went amongst the throng,
    They hewed doon the Hielanmen
    Wi' heavy swords and long.

17 Brave Forbes, he being young and stoot,
    Made the Hielanmen to yield,
    As a scythe doth the green grass
    That grows upon the field.

18 Macdonal, he being young and stoot,
    Had on his coat o' mail,
    And he went swiftly through the ranks
    To fecht wi' him himsel'.

19 The first stroke that Macdonal gave
    He wounded him a dell,
    But the next stroke that brave Forbes gave,
    The proud Macdonal fell.

20 O, there was sic a lamrachie,
    The like you never saw,
    As there was amongst the Hielanmen,
    When they saw Macdonal fa.

21 But when they saw Macdonal fa,
    They lookit lion-like;
    But brave Forbes, wi' his heavy sword,
    He made them fidge and fyke.

19 dell *bit*
20 lamrachie *lament*
21 fidge *fidget* · fyke *caper about*

22 And when they saw their chief was deid,
    Wi' him they ran awa,
And buried him at Leggat's den,
    A lairge mile fae Harlaw.

23 This battle began on Monday,
    Wi' the risin o' the sun,
And on Setterday, at twelve o'clock,
    You would scarce kent fa had won.

24 Oot o' sixty thoosan redcoats
    Went home but thirty-two,
And ninety thoosan Hielanmen
    Went home but forty-three.

25 O, there was sic a burial,
    The like you never saw,
As there was upon the Sabbath day,
    The leas aneath Harlaw.

26 If anyone did ask at you,
    Where's the men you had awa?
Ye may tell him plain and very plain,
    They're sleepin at Harlaw.

25 leas *untilled low ground*

5

Johnnie o' Braidiesleys

1 Johnny arose on a May mornin'
    Called cold water to wash his hands
Says: 'Come lowse to me my good greyhounds
    That lie bound in iron bands
    That lie bound in iron bands.'

2 Johnny shouldered his good bent bow
    His arrows one by one
And he's gane doon by the good greenwood
    For to ding the din deer doon.

3 The din deer lap, and Johnnie fired
    And wounded her on the side
And between the waters, and the woods
    The greyhounds laid her pride.

4 Johnnie skinned his good din deer
    Took out her liver and her lungs
And fed his dogs on the venison
    As gin they were Earl's sons.

5 They ate so much of the venison
    And drank so much of the blood
That they all lay on the plain
    As gin that they were dead.

6 Then by there cam' a silly auld man
    And an ill death may he dee
For he's ga'en doon to Islington
    Where the seven foresters do lie.

2 ding *strike* · din *dun*
3 lap *leapt*
6 silly *simple*

7 Says: 'As I am doon by bonny Monymusk
      An doon among the scrogs
   The fairest youth that ever I saw
      Lay sleepin' amang his dogs.'

8 And then outspake the head forester
      He was forester o'er them a'
   Gin this be Johnny o' Braidiesleys
      It's unto him we'll draw.

9 But then outspake the second forester
      A sister's son was he
   'Gin this be Johnnie Braidiesleys
      We'd better lat him be.'

10 The first shot that the foresters fired
       It wounded him on the knee
    And the second shot that the foresters fired
       His heart's blood blinded his e'e.

11 Now Johnnie awoke him out of his sleep
       And an angry man was he
    Says: 'Ye micht hae awaked me out o' my sleep
       Ere my heart's blood blinded my e'e.

12 'But gin my bent bow prove true to me
       An' seldom it proves wrang
    I'll mak' ye a' rue the day
       That I dang the din deer doon.'

13 He leaned his back against an oak
       His foot against a stone
    And fired at the seven foresters
       An' shot them all but one.

7 scrogs *stunted bushes*
8 draw *go*

14 An' he's broken three of this one's ribs
    Likewise his collar bone
   And laid him twafauld owre a steed
    Bade him carry the tidings home.

15 Johnnie's gude bent bow is broke
    And his twa grey dogs is slain
   And his body lies in Monymusk
    And his huntin' days are dune.

14 twafauld *doubled, with head on one side and feet on the other*

6

Sir Patrick Spens

1 The king sits in Dumfermline town,
   Drinking the blude-red wine: O
  'O whare will I get a skeely skipper,
   To sail this new ship of mine?' O

2 O up and spake an eldern knight,
   Sat at the king's right knee:
  'Sir Patrick Spens is the best sailor
   That ever saild the sea.'

3 Our king has written a braid letter,
   And seald it with his hand,
  And sent it to Sir Patrick Spens,
   Was walking on the strand.

4 'To Noroway, to Noroway,
   To Noroway oer the faem;
  The king's daughter of Noroway,
   'T is thou maun bring her hame.'

1 skeely *skilful*
2 eldern *old*

5 The first word that Sir Patrick read,
     Sae loud, loud laughed he;
  The neist word that Sir Patrick read,
     The tear blinded his ee.

6 'O wha is this has done this deed,
     And tauld the king o me,
  To send us out at this time of the year
     To sail upon the sea?

7 'Be it wind, be it weet, be it hail, be it sleet,
     Our ship must sail the faem;
  The king's daughter of Noroway,
     'T is we must fetch her hame.'

8 They hoysed their sails on Monenday morn,
     Wi a' the speed they may;
  They hae landed in Noroway,
     Upon a Wodensday.

9 They hadna been a week, a week
     In Noroway but twae,
  When that the lords o Noroway
     Began aloud to say:

10 'Ye Scottishmen spend a' our king's goud,
     And a' our queenis fee!'
  'Ye lie, ye lie, ye liars loud,
     Fu loud I hear ye lie!

11 'For I brought as much white monie
     As gane my men and me,
  And I brought a half-fou o gude red goud
     Out oer the sea wi me.

5 neist *next*
10 fee *wealth*
11 white monie *silver* · gane *will suffice* ·
half-fou *bushel*

12 'Make ready, make ready, my merrymen a',
    Our gude ship sails the morn:'
  'Now, ever alake! my master dear,
    I fear a deadly storm!

13 'I saw the new moon late yestreen,
    Wi the auld moon in her arm;
  And if we gang to sea, master,
    I fear we'll come to harm.'

14 They hadna sailed a league, a league,
    A league but barely three,
  When the lift grew dark, and the wind blew loud,
    And gurly grew the sea.

15 The ankers brak, and the topmasts lap,
    It was sic a deadly storm,
  And the waves came oer the broken ship,
    Till a' her sides were torn.

16 'O where will I get a gude sailor,
    To take my helm in hand,
  Till I get up to the tall topmast,
    To see if I can spy land?'

17 'O here am I, a sailor gude,
    To take the helm in hand,
  Till you go up to the tall topmast;
    But I fear you'll neer spy land.'

18 He hadna gane a step, a step,
    A step but barely ane,
  When a bout flew out of our goodly ship,
    And the salt sea it came in.

13 yestreen *last night*
14 lift *sky* · gurly *grim*
15 lap *sprang*
18 bout *bolt*

19 'Gae fetch a web o the silken claith,
    Another o the twine,
And wap them into our ship's side,
    And letna the sea come in.'

20 They fetched a web o the silken claith,
    Another o the twine,
And they wapped them roun that gude ship's side,
    But still the sea came in.

21 O laith, laith were our gude Scots lords
    To weet their cork-heeld shoon;
But lang or a' the play was playd,
    They wat their hats aboon.

22 And mony was the feather-bed
    That flattered on the faem,
And mony was the gude lord's son
    That never mair cam hame.

23 The ladyes wrang their fingers white,
    The maidens tore their hair,
A' for the sake of their true loves,
    For them they'll see na mair.

24 O lang, lang may the ladyes sit,
    Wi their fans into their hand,
Before they see Sir Patrick Spens
    Come sailing to the strand.

25 And lang, lang may the maidens sit,
    Wi their goud kaims in their hair,
A' waiting for their ain dear loves,
    For them they'll see na mair.

19 twine *coarse linen* · wap *stuff*
20 wapped *wrapped*
22 flattered *floated*

26 O forty miles off Aberdeen
    'T is fifty fathoms deep,
And there lies gude Sir Patrick Spens,
    Wi the Scots lords at his feet.

7

The Bonny Earl of Murray

1 Ye Highlands, and ye Lawlands,
    Oh where have you been?
They have slain the Earl of Murray,
    And they layd him on the green.

2 'Now wae be to thee, Huntly!
    And wherefore did you sae?
I bade you bring him wi you,
    But forbade you him to slay.'

3 He was a braw gallant,
    And he rid at the ring;
And the bonny Earl of Murray,
    Oh he might have been a king!

4 He was a braw gallant,
    And he playd at the ba;
And the bonny Earl of Murray
    Was the flower amang them a'.

5 He was a braw gallant,
    And he playd at the glove;
And the bonny Earl of Murray,
    Oh he was the Queen's love!

3 rid at the ring *rode in competition to carry
off a suspended ring on the point of a lance*

6 Oh lang will his lady
    Look oer the castle Down,
Eer she see the Earl of Murray
    Come sounding thro the town!
Eer she, etc.

6 sounding *riding with trumpets blowing*

8

Edom of Gordon

1 It fell about the Martinmas,
    When the wind blew schrile and cauld,
Said Edom o Gordon to his men,
    We maun draw to a hald.

2 'And what an a hald sall we draw to,
    My merry men and me?
We will gae to the house of the Rhodes,
    To see that fair lady.'

3 She had nae sooner busket her sell,
    Nor putten on her gown,
Till Edom o Gordon and his men
    Were round about the town.

4 They had nae sooner sitten down,
    Nor sooner said the grace,
Till Edom o Gordon and his men
    Were closed about the place.

1 Martinmas *11th of November* · schrile *biting* ·
draw to a hald *head for a place of shelter*
2 what an a *which particular*
3 busket *dressed* · town *settlement*

5 The lady ran up to her tower-head,
    As fast as she could drie,
To see if by her fair speeches
    She could with him agree.

6 As soon he saw the lady fair,
    And hir yates all locked fast,
He fell into a rage of wrath,
    And his heart was aghast.

7 'Cum down to me, ye lady fair,
    Cum down to me; let's see;
This night ye's ly by my ain side,
    The morn my bride sall be.'

8 'I winnae cum down, ye fals Gordon,
    I winnae cum down to thee;
I winnae forsake my ane dear lord,
    That is sae far frae me.'

9 'Gi up your house, ye fair lady,
    Gi up your house to me,
Or I will burn yoursel therein,
    Bot and your babies three.'

10 'I winnae gie up, you fals Gordon,
    To nae sik traitor as thee,
Tho you should burn mysel therein,
    Bot and my babies three.'

11 'Set fire to the house,' quoth fals Gordon,
    'Sin better may nae bee;
And I will burn hersel therein,
    Bot and her babies three.'

5 drie *do*
7 the morn *tomorrow*
9 bot and *and also*

12 'And ein wae worth ye, Jock my man!
        I paid ye weil your fee;
    Why pow ye out my ground-wa-stane,
        Lets in the reek to me?

13 'And ein wae worth ye, Jock my man!
        For I paid you weil your hire;
    Why pow ye out my ground-wa-stane,
        To me lets in the fire?'

14 'Ye paid me weil my hire, lady,
        Ye paid me weil my fee,
    But now I'm Edom of Gordon's man,
        Maun either do or die.'

15 O then bespake her youngest son,
        Sat on the nurse's knee,
    'Dear mother, gie owre your house,' he says,
        'For the reek it worries me.'

16 'I winnae gie up my house, my dear,
        To nae sik traitor as he;
    Cum weil, cum wae, my jewels fair,
        Ye maun tak share wi me.'

17 O then bespake her dochter dear,
        She was baith jimp and sma;
    'O row me in a pair o shiets,
        And tow me owre the wa.'

12 ein *even* · wae worth ye *may sorrow come to
you* · pow *pull* · ground-wa-stane *stone at
ground level* · reek *smoke*
14 fee *wages*
15 gie owre *surrender* · worries *chokes*
17 bespake *spoke* · jimp *slender* · row *wrap* ·
tow me *lower me by rope*

18 They rowd her in a pair of shiets,
  And towd her owre the wa,
 But on the point of Edom's speir
  She gat a deadly fa.

19 O bonny, bonny was hir mouth,
  And chirry were her cheiks,
 And clear, clear was hir yellow hair,
  Whereon the reid bluid dreips!

20 Then wi his speir he turnd hir owr;
  O gin hir face was wan!
 He said, You are the first that eer
  I wist alive again.

21 He turned hir owr and owr again;
  O gin hir skin was whyte!
 He said, I might ha spard thy life
  To been some mans delyte.

22 'Busk and boon, my merry men all,
  For ill dooms I do guess;
 I cannae luik in that bonny face,
  As it lyes on the grass.'

23 'Them luiks to freits, my master deir,
  Then freits will follow them;
 Let it neir be said brave Edom o Gordon
  Was daunted with a dame.'

24 O then he spied hir ain deir lord,
  As he came owr the lee;
 He saw his castle in a fire,
  As far as he could see.

20 gin *how* · wist *wished*
22 busk and boon *make ready* · dooms *judgement*
23 them luiks to freits *those who regard omens*
24 lee *grass land*

25 'Put on, put on, my mighty men,
     As fast as ye can drie!
   For he that's hindmost of my men
     Sall neir get guid o me.'

26 And some they raid, and some they ran,
     Fu fast out-owr the plain,
   But lang, lang eer he coud get up
     They were a' deid and slain.

27 But mony were the mudie men
     Lay gasping on the grien;
   For o fifty men that Edom brought out
     There were but five ged heme.

28 And mony were the mudie men
     Lay gasping on the grien,
   And mony were the fair ladys
     Lay lemanless at heme.

29 And round and round the waes he went,
     Their ashes for to view;
   At last into the flames he flew,
     And bad the world adieu.

25 put on *press on* · drie *manage*
26 out-owr *over* · 27 mudie *bold*
28 lemanless *without lovers*
29 waes *walls*

9

The Bonnie Hoose o Airlie

1 It fell on a day, on a bonnie simmer's day
     When the corn was ripe and yellow,
   That there fell oot a great dispute
     Between Argyll and Airlie.

2   Noo the lady looked owre yon high castle waa,
         And oh, but she sighed sairly
     Whan she saa Argyll and aa he's men
         Come tae plunder the bonnie hoose o Airlie.

3   'Come doon, come doon, Lady Marg'ret,' he says,
         'Come doon and kiss me fairly,
     Or gin the mornin's clear daylight
         I'll no leave a stannin stane in Airlie.'

4   'I'll no come doon, you false Argyll,
         Nor wid I kiss thee fairly:
     I widnae kiss the fause Argyll
         Though ye widnae leave a stannin stane in Airlie.

5   'Noo if my guid lord had been at hame
         As he's awaa wi Chairlie,
     There widnae come a Campbell frae Argyll
         Dared tae trod upon the bonnie green o Airlie.

6   'For I have borne him seven bonnie sons
         But the eighth yin has never seen his daddy,
     But had I jist as mony owre again
         They wid aa be men for Chairlie.'

7   Noo Argyll in a rage he kennled sic a lowe
         That it rose tae lift red an clearly,
     An poor Lady Marg'ret and aa her weans
         They were smothered in the dark reek o Airlie.

8   'Draa yir dirks, draa yir dirks!' cried the brave Lochiel;
         'Unsheathe yir swords!' cried Chairlie,
     'An we'll kennle sic a lowe roond the fause Argyll
         An we'll licht it wi a spark oot'n Airlie!'

7 lowe *blaze* · lift *sky* · weans *children* · reek *smoke*

10

The Baron of Brackley

1 In Deeside cam Inverey, whistlin an playin,
    An he was at Brackley's yetts ere the day was dawin,
  'Oh, are ye there, Brackley, an are ye within?
    There's sherp swords are at your yetts, will gar your bluid spin.'

2 'Then rise up, my baron, an turn back yer kye,
    For the lads frae Drumwharran are drivin them by.'
  'Oh, how can I rise up, an how can I gyan,
    For whaur I hae ae man, oh I'm sure they hae ten.

3 'Then rise up, Betsy Gordon, an gie me ma gun,
    An though I gyan oot, love, sure I'll never come in.
  Come, kiss me, ma Betsy, nor think I'm tae blame,
    But against three-an-thirty, wae is me, what a fame.

4 When Brackley was mounted, an rade on his horse,
    A bonnier baron ne'er rade owre a close.
  Twa gallanter Gordons did never sword draw,
    But against three-an-thirty wisnae evens ava.

5 Wi their dirks an their swords they did him surroond,
    An they've slain bonnie Brackley wi monie's the wound.
  Frae the heid o the Dee tae the banks o the Spey,
    The Gordons shall mourn him an ban Inverey.

6 'Oh, come ye by Brackley's yetts, or come ye by here?
    An saw ye his lady, a-rivin her hair?'
  'Oh, I cam by Brackley's yetts, an I cam by here,
    An I saw his fair lady, she was makkin guid cheer.

TITLE baron *owner of a freehold estate*
1 dawin *dawning*
2 kye *cattle* · drivin them by *driving them off* · gyan *go*
4 close *courtyard* · evens *an equal match* · ava *at all*
5 dirks *daggers* · ban *curse*
6 a-rivin *tearing*

7 'She was rantin an dancin an singin for joy
   An she vowed that that nicht she wad feast Inverey.
'She laughed wi him, drank wi him, welcomed him ben;
   She was kind tae the villain had slain her guidman.'

8 'Through hedges an ditches ye canna be sure,
   But through the woods o Glenturner you'll slip in an oor.'
Then up spak the babe on the nanny's knee:
   'It's afore I'm a man avengèd I'll be.'

7 rantin *making merry* · ben *to the inner part of the house*
8 oor *hour*

II

The Gaberlunzie-Man

1 The silly poor Man came o'er the Lee,
   With many Good-day and Good-even to thee,
   Seeking Help for Courtesie,
      O lodge a silly poor Man, *etc.*

2 The Night was cald he was all wet,
   And down beyond the Fire he sate,
   He took the Meal-Pocks off his Back,
      And he began to sing, *etc.*

3 I wish says she I were as white,
   As ever the Snow lay on the Dyke,
   It's I wou'd dress me Lady like,
      And with thee wou'd I gang, *etc.*

1 silly *simple* · lee *grass land*
2 meal-pocks *meal-bags*
3 dyke *wall*

4 O quoth he, and ye were as black,
   As e're the Crown of my Father's Hat,
   You shou'd ly down at my Back,
         And away with you I'd gang, *etc.*

5 And there the two made up the Plot,
   And rose a little before the Cock,
   So cunningly she shut the Lock,
         And to the Fields they're gane, *etc.*

6 Now Staff and Steel to wone thy Bread,
   And Spindle and Whorle to spin a Threed,
   Says she it is a gentle Trade indeed,
         And away with thee I'll gang, *etc.*

7 So in the Morning the Good-wife rose,
   And slowly puts she on her Clothes,
   And to the Servant Lass she goes,
         Where lyes the silly poor Man, *etc.*

8 She went to the Place where the poor Man lay,
   The Sheets was cold, he was away,
   And ay she says a dooleful Day,
         For I fear he's done me harm.

9 Some ran to Coffers some ran to Chist,
   All was there, Nothing was mist;
   And ay she cry'd, Now Thanks be blest,
         For he has done no Harm. *etc.*

10 She went to the Bed where her Daughter lay,
   The Sheets were cold she was away;
   And ay she cry'd, A doolful Day!
         For she's follow'd the Gaberlou[n]zy Man. *etc.*

4 quoth *said*
6 staff *beggar's staff* · steel *needle* · wone *earn* · gentle *noble*
8 dooleful *woeful*
9 coffers *boxes* · chist *chest*

11 Some rode upon Horse, some ran upon Foot,
    The poor Old Wife ran out of her Wit,
    And ay she cries, A doolful Fit!
        She's follow'd the Gaberlounzie Man. *etc.*

12 When Nine Months were come and gone,
    The Begger he came back again,
    Seeking Help, for himself alone,
        As he was a silly poor Man. *etc.*

13 Say[s] she, I love no Begger alone;
    For I had no Daughters, but only one,
    And away with a Begger she has gone,
        And I wist when nor where.

14 I set him down beyond the Fire,
    I gave him all at his Desire,
    And now I may take up my Hire,
        For what I got by him.

15 O Good-wife, what would you give,
    For a Sight of your Daughter alive?
    O false Lown, I fear it's thee
        I wish I had thee slain.

16 No Good-wife, it may not be,
    She's better than I got her from thee,
    She has a Kinshine on her Knee,
        And a Babe into her Wime.

17 As she came riding up the Sand,
    And Four and Twenty at her Hand,
    She was the fairest in the Land;
        And she'll go with the Gaberlounzie Man.

11 out of her wit *mad*
13 wist *knew*
15 lown *rascal*
16 kinshine *child* · wime *womb*

12

Donald of the Isles

1 What wad ye gie to me, mither,
    What wad ye gie to me,
  If I wad gae to Edinbruch city
    And bring hame Lizie Lindsey to thee?

2 'Meikle wad I gie to thee, Donald,
    Meikle wad I gie to thee,
  If ye wad gang to Edinbruch city
    And court her as in povertie.'

3 Whan he cam to Edinbruch city,
    And there a while to resort,
  He called on fair Lizie Lindsey,
    Wha lived at the Canongate-Port.

4 'Will ye gang to the Hielands, Lizie Lindsey?
    Will ye gae to the Hielands wi me?
  And I will gie ye a cup o the curds,
    Likewise a cup of green whey.

5 'And I will gie ye a bed o green threshes,
    Likewise a happing o grey,
  If ye will gae to the Hielands, Lizie Lindsey,
    If ye'll gae to the Hielands wi me.'

6 'How can I gang?' says Lizie Lindsey,
    'How can I gang wi thee?
  I dinna ken whare I am gaing,
    Nor wha I am gaing wi.'

7 'My father is a cowper o cattle,
    My mither is an auld dey;
  My name is Donald Macdonald,
    My name I'll never deny.'

3 resort *reside* · 5 threshes *rushes* · happing *coverlet*
7 cowper o cattle *cattle-dealer* · dey *dairy-woman*

8 Doun cam Lizie Lindsey's father,
   A revrend auld gentleman was he:
'If ye steal awa my dochter,
   Hie hanged ye sall be.'

9 He turned him round on his heel
   And [a] licht lauch gied he:
'There is na law in a' Edinbruch city
   This day that can hang me.'

10 It's doun cam Lizie's hand-maid,
   A bonnie young lass was she:
'If I had ae crown in a' the warld,
   Awa wi that fellow I'd gae.'

11 'Do ye say sae to me, Nelly?
   Do ye say sae to me?
Wad ye leave your father and mither,
   And awa wi that fellow wad gae?'

12 She has kilted her coats o green silk
   A little below her knee,
And she's awa to the Hielands wi Donald,
   To bear him companie.

13 And whan they cam to the vallies
   The hie hills war coverd wi snow,
Which caused monie a saut tear
   From Lizie's een to flow.

14 'O, gin I war in Edinbruch city,
   And safe in my ain countrie,
O, gin I war in Edinbruch city,
   The Hielands shoud never see me.'

10 crown *silver coin worth five shillings*
12 kilted *tucked*

15 'O haud your tongue, Lizie Lindsey,
  Na mair o that let me see;
 I'll tak ye back to Edinbruch city,
  And safe to your ain countrie.'

16 'Though I war in Edinbruch city,
  And safe in my ain countrie,
 Though I war in Edinbruch city,
  O wha wad care for me!'

17 Whan they cam to the shiels o Kilcushneuch,
  Out there cam an auld dey:
 'Ye're welcome here, Sir Donald,
  You and your lady gay.'

18 'Ca me na mair Sir Donald,
  But ca me Donald your son,
 And I'll ca ye my auld mither,
  Till the lang winter nicht is begun.'

19 A' this was spoken in Erse,
  That Lizie micht na ken;
 A' this was spoken in Erse,
  And syne the broad English began.

20 'Ye'll gae and mak to our supper
  A cup o the curds and whey,
 And ye'll mak a bed o green threshes,
  Likewise a happing o grey.'

    ★ ★ ★ ★ ★

21 'Won up, won up, Lizie Lindsey,
  Ye've lain oure lang in the day;
 Ye micht hae been helping my mither
  To milk the ewes and the kye.'

17 shiels *shielings, huts*
19 Erse *Gaelic* · 21 won up *get up*

22 Then up got Lizie Lindsey,
        And the tear blindit her ee:
    'O, gin I war in Edinbruch city
        The Hielands shoud never see me!'

23 'Won up, won up, Lizie Lindsey,
        A fairer sicht ye hae to see;
    Do ye see yon bonnie braw castle?
        Lady o it ye will be.'

13

Johny Faa, the Gypsy Laddie

1 The gypsies came to our good lord's gate,
        And wow but they sang sweetly!
    They sang sae sweet and sae very compleat
        That down came the fair lady.

2 And she came tripping down the stair,
        And a' her maids before her;
    As soon as they saw her well-far'd face,
        They coost the glamer oer her.

3 'Gae tak frae me this gay mantile,
        And bring to me a plaidie;
    For if kith and kin and a' had sworn,
        I'll follow the gypsie laddie.

4 'Yestreen I lay in a well-made bed,
        And my good lord beside me;
    This night I'll ly in a tenant's barn,
        Whatever shall betide me.'

1 compleat *excellently*
2 well-far'd *good-looking* · coost the glamer *cast a spell*
4 yestreen *last night, yesterday*

5 'Come to your bed,' says Johny Faa,
    'Oh come to your bed, my deary;
For I vow and I swear, by the hilt of my sword,
    That your lord shall nae mair come near ye.'

6 'I'll go to bed to my Johny Faa,
    I'll go to bed to my deary;
For I vow and I swear, by what past yestreen,
    That my lord shall nae mair come near me.

7 'I'll mak a hap to my Johnny Faa,
    And I'll mak a hap to my deary;
And he's get a' the coat gaes round,
    And my lord shall nae mair come near me.'

8 And when our lord came hame at een,
    And speir'd for his fair lady,
The tane she cry'd, and the other reply'd,
    'She's away with the gypsie laddie.'

9 'Gae saddle to me the black, black steed,
    Gae saddle and make him ready;
Before that I either eat or sleep,
    I'll gae seek my fair lady.'

10 And we were fifteen well-made men,
    Altho we were nae bonny;
And we were a' put down for ane,
    A fair young wanton lady.

7 hap *wrap*
8 at een *in the evening* · speir'd *asked*
10 put down *put to death, hanged.*

14

The Gowans Sae Gay

1 Fair lady Isabel sits in her bower sewing,
    Aye as the gowans grow gay
There she heard an elf-knight blawing his horn.
    The first morning in May

2 'If I had yon horn that I hear blawing,
And yon elf-knight to sleep in my bosom.'

3 This maiden had scarcely these words spoken,
Till in at her window the elf-knight has luppen.

4 'It's a very strange matter, fair maiden,' said he,
'I canna blaw my horn but ye call on me.

5 'But will ye go to yon greenwood side?
If ye canna gang, I will cause you to ride.'

6 He leapt on a horse, and she on another,
And they rode on to the greenwood together.

7 'Light down, light down, lady Isabel,' said he,
'We are come to the place where ye are to die.

8 'Hae mercy, hae mercy, kind sir, on me,
Till ance my dear father and mother I see.'

9 'Seven king's-daughters here hae I slain,
And ye shall be the eight o them.'

10 'O sit down a while, lay your head on my knee,
That we may hae some rest before that I die.'

11 She stroakd him sae fast, the nearer he did creep,
Wi a sma charm she lulld him fast asleep.

1 gowans *daisies* · 3 luppen *leapt*

12 Wi his ain sword-belt sae fast as she ban him,
    Wi his ain dag-durk sae sair as she dang him.

13 'If seven king's-daughters here ye hae slain,
    Lye ye here, a husband to them a'.'

12 ban *bound* · dag-durk *dagger* · dang *struck*

15

The Wind Hath Blown My Plaid Away

My plaid awa, my plaid awa,
And ore the hill and far awa,
And far awa to Norrowa,
My plaid shall not be blown awa.

1 The elphin knight sits on yon hill,
        Ba, ba, ba, lilli ba
   He blaws his horn both lowd and shril.
        The wind hath blown my plaid awa

2 He blowes it east, he blowes it west,
   He blowes it where he lyketh best.

3 'I wish that horn were in my kist,
   Yea, and the knight in my armes two.'

4 She had no sooner these words said,
   When that the knight came to her bed.

5 'Thou art over young a maid,' quoth he,
   'Married with me thou il wouldst be.'

3 kist *chest*

6   'I have a sister younger than I,
    And she was married yesterday.'

7   'Married with me if thou wouldst be,
    A courtesie thou must do to me.

8   'For thou must shape a sark to me,
    Without any cut or heme,' quoth he.

9   'Thou must shape it knife-and-sheerlesse,
    And also sue it needle-threedlesse.'

10 'If that piece of courtesie I do to thee,
    Another thou must do to me.

11 'I have an aiker of good ley-land,
    Which lyeth low by yon sea-strand.

12 'For thou must eare it with thy horn,
    So thou must sow it with thy corn.

13 'And bigg a cart of stone and lyme,
    Robin Redbreast he must trail it hame.

14 'Thou must barn it in a mouse-holl,
    And thrash it into thy shoes soll.

15 'And thou must winnow it in thy looff,
    And also seck it in thy glove.

16 'For thou must bring it over the sea,
    And thou must bring it dry home to me.

8 sark *shirt* · quoth *said*
9 knife-and-sheerlesse *without knife or scissors*
11 ley-land *uncultivated land* · sea-strand *sea shore*
12 eare *plough* · corn *oats*
13 bigg *build* · trail *draw*
15 looff *hand* · seck *sack*

17 'When thou hast gotten thy turns well done,
   Then come to me and get thy sark then.'

18 'I'l not quite my plaid for my life;
   It haps my seven bairns and my wife.'
   The wind shall not blow my plaid awa

19 'My maidenhead I'l then keep still,
   Let the elphin knight do what he will.'
   The wind's not blown my plaid awa

17 turns *tasks* · 18 quite *quit* · haps *covers*

16

The Earl of Rosslyn's Daughter

1 The Lord of Rosslyn's daughter gaed through the wud her lane,
  And there she met Captain Wedderburn, a servant to the king.
  He said unto his livery-man, Were't na agen the law,
  I wad tak her to my ain bed, and lay her at the wa.

2 'I'm walking here my lane,' she says, 'amang my father's trees;
  And ye may lat me walk my lane, kind sir, now gin ye please.
  The supper-bell it will be rung, and I'll be missd awa;
  Sae I'll na lie in your bed, at neither stock nor wa.'

3 He said, My pretty lady, I pray lend me your hand,
  And ye'll hae drums and trumpets always at your command;
  And fifty men to guard ye wi, that weel their swords can draw;
  Sae we'll baith lie in ae bed, and ye'll lie at the wa.

1 her lane *alone* · livery-man *servant* · 2 stock *outer side*

4 'Haud awa frae me, kind sir, I pray let go my hand;
   The supper-bell it will be rung, nae langer maun I stand.
   My father he'll na supper tak, gif I be missd awa;
   Sae I'll na lie in your bed, at neither stock nor wa.'

5 'O my name is Captain Wedderburn, my name I'll neer deny,
   And I command ten thousand men, upo yon mountains high.
   Tho your father and his men were here, of them I'd stand na awe,
   But should tak ye to my ain bed, and lay ye neist the wa.'

6 Then he lap aff his milk-white steed, and set the lady on,
   And a' the way he walkd on foot, he held her by the hand;
   He held her by the middle jimp, for fear that she should fa;
   Saying, I'll tak ye to my ain bed, and lay thee at the wa.

7 He took her to his quartering-house, his landlady looked ben,
   Saying, Monie a pretty ladie in Edinbruch I've seen;
   But sic 'na pretty ladie is not into it a':
   Gae, mak for her a fine down-bed, and lay her at the wa.

8 'O haud awa frae me, kind sir, I pray ye lat me be,
   For I'll na lie in your bed till I get dishes three;
   Dishes three maun be dressd for me, gif I should eat them a',
   Before I lie in your bed, at either stock or wa.

9 ''T is I maun hae to my supper a chicken without a bane;
   And I maun hae to my supper a cherry without a stane;
   And I maun hae to my supper a bird without a gaw,
   Before I lie in your bed, at either stock or wa.'

10 'Whan the chicken's in the shell, I am sure it has na bane;
   And whan the cherry's in the bloom, I wat it has na stane;
   The dove she is a genty bird, she flees without a gaw;
   Sae we'll baith lie in ae bed, and ye'll be at the wa.'

---

4 haud *keep* · gif *if* · 5 neist *next*
6 lap *leapt* · jimp *slender*
7 quartering-house *lodgings* · ben *within* · sic 'na *such a*
9 gaw *gall* · 10 genty *gentle*

11 'O haud awa frae me, kind sir, I pray ye give me owre,
    For I'll na lie in your bed, till I get presents four;
    Presents four ye maun gie me, and that is twa and twa,
    Before I lie in your bed, at either stock or wa.

12 ''T is I maun hae some winter fruit that in December grew;
    And I maun hae a silk mantil that waft gaed never through;
    A sparrow's horn, a priest unborn, this nicht to join us twa,
    Before I lie in your bed, at either stock or wa.'

13 'My father has some winter fruit that in December grew;
    My mither has a silk mantil the waft gaed never through;
    A sparrow's horn ye soon may find, there's ane on evry claw.
    And twa upo the gab o it, and ye shall get them a'.

14 'The priest he stands without the yett, just ready to come in;
    Nae man can say he eer was born, nae man without he sin;
    He was haill cut frae his mither's side, and frae the same let fa;
    Sae we'll baith lie in ae bed, and ye 'se lie at the wa.'

15 'O haud awa frae me, kind sir, I pray don't me perplex,
    For I'll na lie in your bed till ye answer questions six:
    Questions six ye maun answer me, and that is four and twa,
    Before I lie in your bed, at either stock or wa.

16 'O what is greener than the gress, what's higher than thae trees?
    O what is worse than women's wish, what's deeper than the seas?
    What bird craws first, what tree buds first, what first does on them fa?
    Before I lie in your bed, at either stock or wa.'

17 'Death is greener than the gress, heaven higher than thae trees;
    The devil's waur than women's wish, hell's deeper than the seas;
    The cock craws first, the cedar buds first, dew first on them does fa;
    Sae we'll baith lie in ae bed, and ye 'se lie at the wa.'

12 waft *weft, woof* · 13 gab *mouth* · 16 thae *those* · 17 wish *ill wish, curse*

18 Little did this lady think, that morning whan she raise,
That this was for to be the last o a' her maiden days.
But there's na into the king's realm to be found a blither twa,
And now she's Mrs. Wedderburn, and she lies at the wa.

17

The Unco Knicht's Wouing

1 There was a Knight ridin' frae the East
      Sing the claret banks tae the bonny broom
   Wha had been wooin' at mony a place
      An' ye may beguile a young thing sune

2 He cam' unto a widow's dore
   An' speir'd whare her three dochters war'

3 The auldest ane's tae a washin' gane
   An' the second's tae a bakin' gane

4 The youngest ane's tae a weddin' gane
   An' it will be night ere she be hame

5 He sat him doun upon a stane
   Till these three lasses cam' trippin' hame

6 The auldest ane's tae the bedmakin'
   An' the second ane's tae the sheet spreadin'

7 The youngest ane was bauld an' bright
   An' she was tae lye wi' this unco Knight

8 Gin ye will answere me questions ten
   Tomorrow ye sall be my ain

2 speir'd *enquired* · 7 unco *stranger*

9   O what is heigher than the tree
    An' what is deeper than the sea

10 Or what is heavier than the lead
    Or what is better than the bread

11 O what is whiter than the milk
    Or what is safter than the silk

12 Or what is sharper than a thorn
    Or what is louder than a horn

13 Or what is greener than the grass
    Or what is waur than a woman's wuss

14 O Heav'n is heigher than the tree
    An' Hell is deeper than the sea

15 O sin is heavier than the lead
    The blessing's better than the bread

16 The snaw is whiter than the milk
    An' the down is safter than the silk

17 Hunger's sharper than a thorn
    An' shame is louder than a horn

18 The Peas are greener than the grass
    An' the Fiend is waur than a woman's wuss

19 As sune as she the Fiend did name
    He flew awa in a fierie flame

    13 wuss *wish, curse*

18

The Fause Knicht

1 O whar are ye gaun?
      Quo the fause knicht upon the road.
   I'm gawn to the skeul,
      Quo the wee boy and still he stood.

2 What is that upon your back?
   Atweel it is my books.

3 What's that ye hae gotten in your arm?
   Atweel it is my peat.

4 Wha's aught they sheep?
   They are mine an my mother's.

5 How money of them are mine?
   Aw them that hae blue tails.

6 O I wish ye were on yon tree.
   And a guid ladder under me.

7 And the ladder for to break.
   And you for to faw down.

8 I wish ye were in yon sea.
   And a gude bottom under me.

9 And the bottom for to break.
   And you for to be drowned.

1 quo *said*
2 atweel *certainly, sure*
3 peat *piece of peat (for use on the
schoolroom fire)*
4 wha's aught they sheep *whose are
these sheep*
8 bottom *ship*

19

The Daemon Lover

1   'O where have you been, my long, long love,
       This long seven years and mair?'
    'O I'm come to seek my former vows
       Ye granted me before.'

2   'O hold your tongue of your former vows,
       For they will breed sad strife;
    O hold your tongue of your former vows,
       For I am become a wife.'

3   He turned him right and round about,
       And the tear blinded his ee:
    'I wad never hae trodden on Irish ground,
       If it had not been for thee.

4   'I might hae had a king's daughter,
       Far, far beyond the sea;
    I might have had a king's daughter,
       Had it not been for love o thee.'

5   'If ye might have had a king's daughter,
       Yer sel ye had to blame;
    Ye might have taken the king's daughter,
       For ye kend that I was nane.

6   'If I was to leave my husband dear,
       And my two babes also,
    O what have you to take me to,
       If with you I should go?'

7   'I hae seven ships upon the sea —
       The eighth brought me to land —
    With four-and-twenty bold mariners,
       And music on every hand.'

8 She has taken up her two little babes,
     Kissd them baith cheek and chin:
'O fair ye weel, my ain two babes,
     For I'll never see you again.'

9 She set her foot upon the ship,
     No mariners could she behold;
But the sails were o the taffetie,
     And the masts o the beaten gold.

10 She had not sailed a league, a league,
     A league but barely three,
When dismal grew his countenance,
     And drumlie grew his ee.

11 They had not saild a league, a league,
     A league but barely three,
Until she espied his cloven foot,
     And she wept right bitterlie.

12 'O hold your tongue of your weeping,' says he,
     'Of your weeping now let me be;
I will shew you how the lilies grow
     On the banks of Italy.'

13 'O what hills are yon, yon pleasant hills,
     That the sun shines sweetly on?'
'O yon are the hills of heaven,' he said,
     'Where you will never win.'

14 'O whaten a mountain is yon,' she said,
     'All so dreary wi frost and snow?'
'O yon is the mountain of hell,' he cried,
     'Where you and I will go.'

10 drumlie *gloomy* · 13 win *arrive*

15 He strack the tap-mast wi his hand,
    The fore-mast wi his knee,
  And he brake that gallant ship in twain,
    And sank her in the sea.

20

Burd Ellen

1 'I warn ye all, ye gay ladies,
    That wear scarlet an brown,
  That ye dinna leave your father's house,
    To follow young men frae town.'

2 'O here am I, a lady gay,
    That wears scarlet an brown,
  Yet I will leave my father's house,
    An follow Lord John frae the town.'

3 Lord John stood in his stable-door,
    Said he was bound to ride;
  Burd Ellen stood in her bowr-door,
    Said she'd rin by his side.

4 He's pitten on his cork-heeld shoone,
    An fast awa rade he;
  She's clade hersel in page array,
    An after him ran she.

5 Till they came till a wan water,
    An folks do ca it Clyde;
  Then he's lookit oer his left shoulder,
    Says, Lady, can ye wide?

3 bound *ready* · 5 wide *wade*

6 'O I learnt it i my father house,
   An I learnt it for my weal,
Wenneer I came to a wan water,
   To swim like ony eel.'

7 But the firstin stap the lady stappit,
   The water came til her knee;
'Ohon, alas!' said the lady,
   'This water's oer deep for me.'

8 The nextin stap the lady stappit,
   The water came till her middle;
An sighin says that gay lady,
   I've wat my gouden girdle

9 The nextin stap the lady stappit,
   The water came till her pap;
An the bairn that was in her twa side
   For caul begane to quake.

10 'Lye still, lye still, my ain dear babe,
   Ye work your mither wae;
Your father rides on high horse-back,
   Cares little for us twae.'

11 O about the midst o Clyden water
   There was a yeard-fast stane;
He lightly turnd his horse about,
   An took her on him behin.

12 'O tell me this now, good Lord John,
   An a word ye dinna lee,
How far it is to your lodgin,
   Whare we this night maun be?'

9 pap *breast*
11 yeard-fast *fixed firmly in the ground*

13 'O see you nae yon castle, Ellen,
       That shines sae fair to see?
   There is a lady in it, Ellen,
       Will sunder you an me.

14 'There is a lady in that castle
       Will sunder you and I:'
   'Betide me well, betide me wae,
       I sal go there an try.'

15 'O my dogs sal eat the good white bread,
       An ye sal eat the bran;
   Then will ye sigh, an say, alas!
       That ever I was a man!'

16 'O I sal eat the good white bread,
       An your dogs sal eat the bran;
   An I hope to live an bless the day,
       That ever ye was a man.'

17 'O my horse sal eat the good white meal,
       An ye sal eat the corn;
   Then will ye curse the heavy hour
       That ever your love was born.'

18 'O I sal eat the good white meal,
       An your horse sal eat the corn;
   An I ay sall bless the happy hour
       That ever my love was born.'

19 O four an twenty gay ladies
       Welcomd Lord John to the ha,
   But a fairer lady than tham a'
       Led his horse to the stable sta.

15 bran *husks*

20 An four an twenty gay ladies
    Welcomd Lord John to the green,
But a fairer lady than them a'
    At the manger stood alane.

21 Whan bells were rung, an mass was sung,
    An a' men boun to meat,
Burd Ellen at a bye-table
    Amo the foot-men was set.

22 'O eat an drink, my bonny boy,
    The white bread an the beer:'
'The never a bit can I eat or drink,
    My heart's sae full of fear.'

23 'O eat an drink, my bonny boy,
    The white bread an the wine:'
'O I canna eat nor drink, master,
    My heart's sae full of pine.'

24 But out it spake Lord John's mother,
    An a wise woman was she:
'Whare met ye wi that bonny boy,
    That looks sae sad on thee?

25 'Sometimes his cheek is rosy red,
    An sometimes deadly wan;
He's liker a woman big wi bairn,
    Than a young lord's serving man.'

26 'O it makes me laugh, my mother dear,
    Sic words to hear frae thee;
He is a squire's ae dearest son,
    That for love has followd me.

21 boun to meat *prepared to eat a meal*
bye-table *side table*
23 pine *pain*

27 'Rise up, rise up, my bonny boy,
    Gi my horse corn an hay:'
'O that I will, my master dear,
    As quickly as I may.'

28 She's taen the hay under her arm,
    The corn intill her han,
An she's gane to the great stable,
    As fast as eer she can.

29 'O room ye roun, my bonny broun steeds,
    O room ye near the wa;
For the pain that strikes me thro my sides
    Full soon will gar me fa.'

30 She's leand her back against the wa;
    Strong travail seizd her on;
An even amo the great horse feet
    Burd Ellen brought forth her son.

31 Lord John'[s] mither intill her bowr
    Was sitting all alone,
Whan, i the silence o the night,
    She heard fair Ellen's moan.

32 'Won up, won up, my son,' she says,
    'Go se how a' does fare;
For I think I hear a woman's groans,
    An a bairn greeting sair.'

33 O hastily he gat him up,
    Stayd neither for hose nor shoone,
An he's doen him to the stable-door,
    Wi the clear light o the moon.

29 room ye roun *move round so as to make room*
30 travail *birth pangs*
32 won up *get up*
33 doen him *gone*

34 He strack the door hard wi his foot,
    An sae has he wi his knee,
An iron locks an iron bars
    Into the floor flung he:
'Be not afraid, Burd Ellen,' he says,
    'Ther's nane come in but me.'

35 Up he has taen his bonny young son,
    An gard wash him wi the milk;
An up has he taen his fair lady,
    Gard row her in the silk.

36 'Cheer up your heart, Burd Ellen,' he says,
    'Look nae mair sad nor wae;
For your marriage an your kirkin too
    Sal baith be in ae day.'

36 kirkin *churching*

2I

The Place Where My Love
Johnny Dwells

I The sun shines high on yonder hill,
    And low on yonder town;
In the place where my love Johnny dwells,
    The sun gaes never down.

2 'O when will ye be back, bonny lad,
    O when will ye be hame?'
'When heather-hills are nine times brunt,
    And a' grown green again.'

2 brunt *burnt*

3   'O that's ower lang awa, bonny lad,
        O that's ower lang frae hame;
    For I'll be dead and in my grave
        Ere ye come back again.'

4   He put his foot into the stirrup
        And said he maun go ride,
    But she kilted up her green claithing
        And said she woudna bide.

5   The firsten town that they came to,
        He bought her hose and sheen,
    And bade her rue and return again,
        And gang nae farther wi him.

6   'Ye likena me at a', bonny lad,
        Ye likena me at a'';'
    'It's sair for you likes me sae weel
        And me nae you at a'.'

7   The nexten town that they came to,
        He bought her a braw new gown,
    And bade her rue and return again,
        And gang nae farther wi him.

8   The nexten town that they came to,
        He bought her a wedding ring,
    And bade her dry her rosy cheeks,
        And he would tak her wi him.

9   'O wae be to your bonny face,
        And your twa blinkin een!
    And wae be to your rosy cheeks!
        They've stown this heart o mine.

4 kilted *tucked* · bide *remain behind*
9 blinkin *sparkling* · stown *stolen*

10 'There's comfort for the comfortless,
  There's honey for the bee;
There's comfort for the comfortless,
  There's nane but you for me.'

22

Young Bicham

1 In London city was Bicham born,
  He longd strange countries for to see,
But he was taen by a savage Moor,
  Who handld him right cruely.

2 For thro his shoulder he put a bore,
  An thro the bore has pitten a tree,
An he's gard him draw the carts o wine,
  Where horse and oxen had wont to be.

3 He's casten [him] in a dungeon deep,
  Where he coud neither hear nor see;
He's shut him up in a prison strong,
  An he's handld him right cruely.

4 O this Moor he had but ae daughter,
  I wot her name was Shusy Pye;
She's doen her to the prison-house,
  And she's calld Young Bicham one word by.

5 'O hae ye ony lands or rents,
  Or citys in your ain country,
Coud free you out of prison strong,
  An coud mantain a lady free?'

2 bore *hole* · tree *shaft* · had wont *were accustomed*
4 doen her *gone*

[88]

6 'O London city is my own,
      An other citys twa or three,
  Coud loose me out o prison strong,
      An coud mantain a lady free.'

7 O she has bribed her father's men
      Wi meikle goud and white money,
  She's gotten the key o the prison doors,
      An she has set Young Bicham free.

8 She's gi'n him a loaf o good white bread,
      But an a flask o Spanish wine,
  An she bad him mind on the ladie's love
      That sae kindly freed him out o pine.

9 'Go set your foot on good ship-board,
      An haste you back to your ain country,
  An before that seven years has an end,
      Come back again, love, and marry me.'

10 It was long or seven years had an end
      She longd fu sair her love to see;
  She's set her foot on good ship-board,
      An turnd her back on her ain country.

11 She's saild up, so has she doun,
      Till she came to the other side;
  She's landed at Young Bicham's gates,
      An I hop this day she sal be his bride.

12 'Is this Young Bicham's gates?' says she,
      'Or is that noble prince within?'
  'He's up the stairs wi his bonny bride,
      An monny a lord and lady wi him.'

7 white money *silver*
8 mind on *remember* · pine *suffering*
10 or *before*

13 'O has he taen a bonny bride,
    An has he clean forgotten me!'
An sighing said that gay lady,
    I wish I were in my ain country!

14 But she's pitten her han in her pocket,
    An gin the porter guineas three;
Says, Take ye that, ye proud porter,
    An bid the bridegroom speak to me.

15 O whan the porter came up the stair,
    He's fa'n low down upon his knee:
'Won up, won up, ye proud porter,
    An what makes a' this courtesy?'

16 'O I've been porter at your gates
    This mair nor seven years an three,
But there is a lady at them now
    The like of whom I never did see.

17 'For on every finger she has a ring,
    An on the mid-finger she has three,
An there's as meikle goud aboon her brow
    As woud buy an earldome o lan to me.'

18 Then up it started Young Bicham,
    An sware so loud by Our Lady,
'It can be nane but Shusy Pye,
    That has come oer the sea to me.'

19 O quickly ran he down the stair,
    O fifteen steps he has made but three;
He's tane his bonny love in his arms,
    An a wot he kissd her tenderly.

15 won up *get up*

20 'O hae you tane a bonny bride?
  An hae you quite forsaken me?
 An hae ye quite forgotten her
  That gae you life an liberty?'

21 She's lookit oer her left shoulder
  To hide the tears stood in her ee;
 'Now fare thee well, Young Bicham,' she says,
  'I'll strive to think nae mair on thee.'

22 'Take back your daughter, madam,' he says,
  'An a double dowry I'll gi her wi;
 For I maun marry my first true love,
  That's done and suffered so much for me.'

23 He's take his bonny love by the han,
  And led her to yon fountain stane;
 He's changd her name frae Shusy Pye,
  An he's cald her his bonny love, Lady Jane.

23

Hind Horn

1 In Scotland there was a babie born,
  Lill lal, etc.
And his name it was called young Hind Horn.
  With a fal lal, etc.

2 He sent a letter to our king
 That he was in love with his daughter Jean.

3 He's gien to her a silver wand,
 With seven living lavrocks sitting thereon.

3 lavrocks *larks*

4   She's gien to him a diamond ring,
    With seven bright diamonds set therein.

5   'When this ring grows pale and wan,
    You may know by it my love is gane.'

6   One day as he looked his ring upon,
    He saw the diamonds pale and wan.

7   He left the sea and came to land,
    And the first that he met was an old beggar man.

8   'What news, what news?' said young Hind Horn;
    'No news, no news,' said the old beggar man.

9   'No news,' said the beggar, 'no news at a',
    But there is a wedding in the king's ha.

10 'But there is a wedding in the king's ha,
    That has halden these forty days and twa.'

11 'Will ye lend me your begging coat?
    And I'll lend you my scarlet cloak.

12 'Will you lend me your beggar's rung?
    And I'll gie you my steed to ride upon.

13 'Will you lend me your wig o hair,
    To cover mine, because it is fair?'

14 The auld beggar man was bound for the mill,
    But young Hind Horn for the king's hall.

15 The auld beggar man was bound for to ride,
    But young Hind Horn was bound for the bride.

10 halden *lasted* · 12 rung *staff* · 15 bound *ready*

16   When he came to the king's gate,
      He sought a drink for Hind Horn's sake.

17   The bride came down with a glass of wine,
      When he drank out the glass, and dropt in the ring.

18   'O got ye this by sea or land?
      Or got ye it off a dead man's hand?'

19   'I got not it by sea, I got it by land,
      And I got it, madam, out of your own hand.'

20   'O I'll cast off my gowns of brown,
      And beg wi you frae town to town.

21   'O I'll cast off my gowns of red,
      And I'll beg wi you to win my bread.'

22   'Ye needna cast off your gowns of brown,
      For I'll make you lady o many a town.

23   'Ye needna cast off your gowns of red,
      It's only a sham, the begging o my bread.'

24   The bridegroom he had wedded the bride,
      But young Hind Horn he took her to bed.

17 drank out the glass *drank all the contents of the glass*

Katharine Jaffray

1 There livd a lass in yonder dale,
     And doun in yonder glen, O
And Kathrine Jaffray was her name,
     Well known by many men. O

2 Out came the Laird of Lauderdale,
     Out frae the South Countrie,
All for to court this pretty maid,
     Her bridegroom for to be.

3 He has teld her father and mither baith,
     And a' the rest o her kin,
And has teld the lass hersell,
     And her consent has win.

4 Then came the Laird of Lochinton,
     Out frae the English border,
All for to court this pretty maid,
     Well mounted in good order.

5 He's teld her father and mither baith,
     As I hear sindry say,
But he has nae teld the lass her sell,
     Till on her wedding day.

6 When day was set, and friends were met,
     And married to be,
Lord Lauderdale came to the place,
     The bridal for to see.

7 'O are you came for sport, young man:
     Or are you come for play?
Or are you come for a sight o our bride,
     Just on her wedding day?'

5 sindry *sundry people*

8 'I'm nouther come for sport,' he says,
      'Nor am I come for play;
   But if I had one sight o your bride,
      I'll mount and ride away.'

9 There was a glass of the red wine
      Filld up them atween,
   And ay she drank to Lauderdale,
      Wha her true-love had been.

10 Then he took her by the milk-white hand,
      And by the grass-green sleeve,
   And he mounted her high behind him there,
      At the bridegroom he askt nae leive.

11 Then the blude run down by the Cowden Banks,
      And down by Cowden Braes,
   And ay she gard the trumpet sound,
      'O this is foul, foul play!'

12 Now a' ye that in England are,
      Or are in England born,
   Come nere to Scotland to court a lass,
      Or else ye'l get the scorn.

13 They haik ye up and settle ye by,
      Till on your wedding day,
   And gie ye frogs instead o fish,
      And play ye foul, foul play.

12 get the scorn *be put to shame by rejection*
13 haik ye up and settle ye by *delude you with false hopes and set you aside*

25

Lord Thomas and Fair Annie

1 'It's narrow, narrow, make your bed,
And learn to lie your lane;
For I'm ga'n oer the sea, Fair Annie,
A braw bride to bring hame.
Wi her I will get gowd and gear;
Wi you I neer got nane.

2 'But wha will bake my bridal bread,
Or brew my bridal ale?
And wha will welcome my brisk bride,
That I bring oer the dale?'

3 'It's I will bake your bridal bread,
And brew your bridal ale,
And I will welcome your brisk bride,
That you bring oer the dale.'

4 'But she that welcomes my brisk bride
Maun gang like maiden fair;
She maun lace on her robe sae jimp,
And braid her yellow hair.'

5 'But how can I gang maiden-like,
When maiden I am nane?
Have I not born seven sons to thee,
And am with child again?'

6 She's taen her young son in her arms,
Another in her hand,
And she's up to the highest tower,
To see him come to land.

1 your lane *alone* · 4 jimp *neat*

7   'Come up, come up, my eldest son,
      And look oer yon sea-strand,
  And see your father's new-come bride,
      Before she come to land.'

8   'Come down, come down, my mother dear,
      Come frae the castle wa!
  I fear, if langer ye stand there,
      Ye'll let yoursell down fa.'

9   And she gaed down, and farther down,
      Her love's ship for to see,
  And the topmast and the mainmast
      Shone like the silver free.

10   And she's gane down, and farther down,
      The bride's ship to behold,
  And the topmast and the mainmast
      They shone just like the gold.

11   She's taen her seven sons in her hand,
      I wot she didna fail;
  She met Lord Thomas and his bride,
      As they came oer the dale.

12   'You're welcome to your house, Lord Thomas,
      You're welcome to your land;
  You're welcome with your fair ladye,
      That you lead by the hand.

13   'You're welcome to your ha's, ladye,
      Your welcome to your bowers;
  You're welcome to your hame, ladye,
      For a' that's here is yours.'

9 free *precious*

14 'I thank thee, Annie; I thank thee, Annie,
    Sae dearly as I thank thee;
You're the likest to my sister Annie,
    That ever I did see.

15 'There came a knight out oer the sea,
    And steald my sister away;
The shame scoup in his company,
    And land whereer he gae!'

16 She hang ae napkin at the door,
    Another in the ha,
And a' to wipe the trickling tears,
    Sae fast as they did fa.

17 And aye she served the lang tables,
    With white bread and with wine,
And aye she drank the wan water,
    To had her colour fine.

18 And aye she served the lang tables,
    With white bread and with brown;
And ay she turned her round about,
    Sae fast the tears fell down.

19 And he's taen down the silk napkin,
    Hung on a silver pin,
And aye he wipes the tear trickling
    A' down her cheek and chin.

20 And aye he turn'd him round about,
    And smiled amang his men;
Says, Like ye best the old ladye,
    Or her that's new come hame?

15 shame scoup *Devil fly*
17 had *keep* · fine *delicate*
19 pin *peg*

21 When bells were rung, and mass was sung,
    And a' men bound to bed,
Lord Thomas and his new-come bride
    To their chamber they were gaed.

22 Annie made her bed a little forbye,
    To hear what they might say;
'And ever alas!' Fair Annie cried,
    'That I should see this day!

23 'Gin my seven sons were seven young rats,
    Running on the castle wa,
And I were a grey cat mysell,
    I soon would worry them a'.

24 'Gin my seven sons were seven young hares,
    Running oer yon lilly lee,
And I were a grew hound mysell,
    Soon worried they a' should be.'

25 And wae and sad Fair Annie sat,
    And drearie was her sang,
And ever, as she sobbd and grat,
    'Wae to the man that did the wrang!'

26 'My gown is on,' said the new-come bride,
    'My shoes are on my feet,
And I will to Fair Annie's chamber,
    And see what gars her greet.

27 'What ails ye, what ails ye, Fair Annie,
    That ye make sic a moan?
Has your wine barrels cast the girds,
    Or is your white bread gone?

21 bound *gone* · 22 a little forbye *near by*
23 worry *kill by attacking throat*
24 lilly lee *lovely plain* · grew hound *greyhound*
25 wae *woeful* · 27 cast the girds *lost their hoops*

[99]

28 'O wha was 't was your father, Annie,
     Or wha was 't was your mother?
   And had ye ony sister, Annie,
     Or had ye ony brother?'

29 'The Earl of Wemyss was my father,
     The Countess of Wemyss my mother;
   And a' the folk about the house
     To me were sister and brother.'

30 'If the Earl of Wemyss was your father,
     I wot sae was he mine;
   And it shall not be for lack o gowd
     That ye your love sall tyne.

31 'For I have seven ships o mine ain,
     A' loaded to the brim,
   And I will gie them a' to thee,
     Wi four to thine eldest son:
   But thanks to a' the powers in heaven
     That I gae maiden hame!'

30 tyne *lose*

26

Wee Messgrove

1 Lord Barnard's awa to the green wood,
     To hunt the fallow deer;
   His vassals a' are gane wi him,
     His companie to bear.

2 His lady wrate a braid letter,
     And seald it wi her hand,
   And sent it aff to Wee Messgrove,
     To come at her command.

3 When Messgrove lookt the letter on,
    A waefu man was he;
  Sayin, Gin I'm gript wi Lord Barnard's wife,
    Sure hanged I will be.

4 When he came to Lord Barnard's castel
    He tinklit at the ring,
  And nane was so ready as the lady hersell
    To let Wee Messgrove in.

5 'Welcome, welcome, Messgrove,' she said,
    'You're welcome here to me;
  Lang hae I loed your bonnie face,
    And lang hae ye loed me.

6 'Lord Barnard is a hunting gane,
    I hope he'll neer return,
  And ye sall sleep into his bed,
    And keep his lady warm.'

7 'It cannot be,' Messgrove he said,
    'I ween it cannot be;
  Gin Lord Barnard suld come hame this nicht,
    What wuld he do to me?'

8 'Ye naething hae to fear, Messgrove,
    Ye naething hae to fear;
  I'll set my page without the gate,
    To watch till morning clear.'

9 But wae be to the wee fut-page,
    And an ill death mat he die!
  For he's awa to the green wood,
    As hard as he can flee.

3 gript *taken*
5 loed *loved*
9 mat *may*

10 And whan he to the green wood cam,
  'T was dark as dark could bee,
 And he fand his maister and his men
  Asleep aneth a tree.

11 'Rise up, rise up, maister,' he said,
  'Rise up, and speak to me;
 Your wife's in bed wi Wee Messgrove,
  Rise up richt speedilie.'

12 'Gin that be true ye tell to me,
  A lord I will mak thee;
 But gin it chance to be a lie,
  Sure hanged ye sall be.'

13 'It is as true, my lord,' he said,
  'As ever ye were born;
 Messgrove's asleep in your lady's bed,
  All for to keep her warm.'

14 He mounted on his milk-white steed,
  He was ane angry man;
 And he reachd his stately castell gate
  Just as the day did dawn.

15 He put his horn unto his mouth,
  And he blew strong blasts three;
 Sayin, He that's in bed with anither man's wife,
  He suld be gaun awa.

16 Syne out and spak the Wee Messgrove,
  A frichtit man was he;
 'I hear Lord Barnard's horn,' he said,
  'It blaws baith loud and hie.'

17 'Lye still, lye still, my Wee Messgrove,
  And keep me frae the cauld;
 'T is but my father's shepherd's horn,
  A sounding in the fauld.'

18 He put his horn unto his mouth,
  And he blew loud blasts three;
 Saying, He that's in bed wi anither man's wife,
  'T is time he was awa.

19 Syne out and spak the Wee Messgrove,
  A frichtit man was he:
 'Yon surely is Lord Barnard's horn,
  And I maun een gae flee.'

20 'Lye still, lye still, Messgrove,' she said,
  'And keep me frae the cauld;
 'T is but my father's shepherd's horn,
  A sounding in the fauld.'

21 And ay Lord Barnard blew and blew,
  Till he was quite wearie;
 Syne he threw down his bugle horn,
  And up the stair ran he.

22 'How do you like my blankets, Sir?
  How do you like my sheets?
 How do ye like my gay ladie,
  That lies in your arms asleep?'

23 'Oh weel I like your blankets, Sir,
  And weel I like your sheet;
 But wae be to your gay ladie,
  That lyes in my arms asleep!'

24 'I'll gie you ae sword, Messgrove,
  And I will take anither;
 What fairer can I do, Messgrove,
  Altho ye war my brither?'

19 een *even*

25 The firsten wound that Messgrove gat,
       It woundit him richt sair;
   And the second wound that Messgrove gat,
       A word he neer spak mair.

26 'Oh how do ye like his cheeks, ladie?
       Or how do ye like his chin?
   Or how do ye like his fair bodie,
       That there's nae life within?'

27 'Oh weel I like his cheeks,' she said,
       'And weel I like his chin;
   And weel I like his fair bodie,
       That there's nae life within.'

28 'Repeat these words, my fair ladie,
       Repeat them ower agane,
   And into a basin of pure silver
       I'll gar your heart's bluid rin.'

29 'Oh weel I like his cheeks,' she said,
       'And weel I like his chin;
   And better I like his fair bodie
       Than a' your kith and kin.'

30 Syne he took up his gude braid sword,
       That was baith sharp and fine,
   And into a basin of pure silver
       Her heart's bluid he gart rin.

31 'O wae be to my merrie men,
       And wae be to my page,
   That they didna hald my cursed hands
       When I was in a rage!'

29 kith and kin *friends and relations*

32 He leand the halbert on the ground,
    The point o 't to his breast,
Saying, Here are three sauls gaun to heaven,
    I hope they'll a' get rest.

32 halbert *spear incorporating an axe-blade*

27

Bob Norris

1 Bob Norris is to the grein wud gane
    He's awa wi the wun
His horse is silver shod afore
    In the shynand gowd ahin

2 He said unto his little boy John
    I see what ye dinna see
I see the first woman that I eir luvit
    Or ever luvit me

3 Gae tack to her this pair o gluves
    Thay'r o the sillar grey
An tell her to cum to the merrie grein wud
    An speik to Bob Norrise

4 Gae tack to her this gay gowd ring
    Its aw gowd but the stane
An tell her to cum to the merrie grein wud
    An ask the leive of nane

5 Gae tack to her this gay manteil
    It's aw silk but the sleive
An tell her to cum to the merrie grein wud
    An ask nae bauld baron's leive

6 I daur na gang to Lord Barnard's haw
      I daur na gang for my lyfe
  I daur na gang to Lord Barnard's castle
      To deprive him o' his wyfe

7 Do I nae pay you gowd he said
      Do I nae pay you fee
  How daur you staun my bidding Sir
      Whan I bid you to flee

8 Gif I maun gang to Lord Barnard's castle
      Sae sair agane my wull
  I vow a vow an I doublie vow
      It sall be dune for ill

9 But whan he cam to Lord Barnard's castle
      He tinklit at the ring
  Tha war nane sae reddy as Lord Barnard himsel
      To let the little boy in

10 What news quhat news my bonnie wee boy
      What news hae ye to me
  Nae news nae news Lord Barnard he said
      But your ladie I fain wad see

11 Here is a pair o gluves to her
      Thay'r o' the sillar gray
  An tell her to cum to the merrie grein wud
      An speik to Bob Norris

12 Here is a gay gowd ring to her
      It's aw gowd but the stane
  An sho maun cum to the merrie grein wud
      An ask the leive o' nane

7 staun *withstand*
9 tha *there*
10 fain wad *would like to*

13　Here is a gay manteil to her
　　　　Its aw silk but the sleive
　　An she maun cum to the merrie grein wud
　　　　An ask nae bauld baron's leive

14　Than out bespak the yellow nurse
　　　　Wi the babie on her knie
　　Sayand gif thay be cum frae Bob Norris
　　　　Thay'r welcum unto me

15　O haud your tung ye yellow nurse
　　　　Aloud an I heir ye lie
　　For thay'r to Lord Barnard's ladie
　　　　I trew that this be sho

16　Lord Barnard's to a dressing room gane
　　　　An buskt him in women's array
　　An he's awa to the merrie grein wud
　　　　To speik to Bob Norris

17　Bob Norris he sits on a trie
　　　　He was whistling an singing
　　Said — merrie merrie may my hart be
　　　　I see my mither cumand

18　Bob Norris he cam doun frae the trie
　　　　To help his mither off the horse
　　But alace, alace, says Bob Norris
　　　　My mither was neir sae gross

19　Lord Barnard liftit his nutbrown swurd
　　　　That hang down by his knie
　　An he has cut Bob Norris's heid
　　　　Aff frae his fair bodie

15 trew *believe* · 16 buskt him *got dressed*

20 He tock the bluidie heid in his haun
    An broucht it to the haw
An flang it into his ladie's lap
    Sayand lady thare's a baw

21 Sho tock the bluidie heid in her haun
    An kissit it frae cheik to chin
Sayand Better I lyke that weil faurit face
    Than aw my royal kin

22 Whan I was in my faither's bour
    Aw in my dignitie
An English Lord a visit cam
    Got Bob Norris wi me

23 Than out bespak Lord Barnard than
    An a sorrie man was he
Sayand gif I had kennit that he was your son
    He wad neir been killit be me.

21 weil faurit *handsome* · 23 bespak *spoke*

28

Lord Thomas and Fair Annet

1 Lord Thomas and Fair Annet
    Sate a' day on a hill;
Whan night was cum, and sun was sett,
    They had not talkt their fill.

2 Lord Thomas said a word in jest,
    Fair Annet took it ill:
'A, I will nevir wed a wife
    Against my ain friends' will.'

2 friends' *relations'*

3 'Gif ye wull nevir wed a wife,
    A wife wull neir wed yee:'
Sae he is hame to tell his mither,
    And knelt upon his knee.

4 'O rede, O rede, mither,' he says,
    'A gude rede gie to mee;
O sall I tak the nut-browne bride,
    And let Faire Annet bee?'

5 'The nut-browne bride haes gowd and gear,
    Fair Annet she has gat nane;
And the little beauty Fair Annet haes
    O it wull soon be gane.'

6 And he has till his brother gane:
    'Now, brother, rede ye mee;
A, sall I marrie the nut-browne bride,
    And let Fair Annet bee?'

7 'The nut-browne bride has oxen, brother,
    The nut-browne bride has kye;
I wad hae ye marrie the nut-browne bride,
    And cast Fair Annet bye.'

8 'Her oxen may dye i the house, billie,
    And her kye into the byre,
And I sall hae nothing to mysell
    Bot a fat fadge by the fyre.'

9 And he has till his sister gane:
    'Now, sister, rede ye mee;
O sall I marrie the nut-browne bride,
    And set Fair Annet free?'

4 rede *advise* · a gude rede gie to mee *give me a
good piece of advice*
7 kye *cattle*
8 billie *brother* · byre *cow-house* · fadge *dumpy
person*

10 'I'se rede ye tak Fair Annet, Thomas,
    And let the browne bride alane;
  Lest ye sould sigh, and say, Alace,
    What is this we brought hame!'

11 'No, I will tak my mither's counsel,
    And marrie me owt o hand;
  And I will tak the nut-browne bride,
    Fair Annet may leive the land.'

12 Up then rose Fair Annet's father,
    Twa hours or it wer day,
  And he is gane into the bower
    Wherein Fair Annet lay.

13 'Rise up, rise up, Fair Annet,' he says,
    'Put on your silken sheene;
  Let us gae to St. Marie's kirke,
    And see that rich weddeen.'

14 'My maides, gae to my dressing-roome,
    And dress to me my hair;
  Whaireir yee laid a plait before,
    See yee lay ten times mair.

15 'My maids, gae to my dressing-room,
    And dress to me my smock;
  The one half is o the holland fine,
    The other o needle-work.'

16 The horse Fair Annet rade upon,
    He amblit like the wind;
  Wi siller he was shod before,
    Wi burning gowd behind.

11 owt o hand *immediately*
12 or *before*
15 holland *linen*

17 Four and twanty siller bells
        Wer a' tyed till his mane,
    And yae tift o the norland wind,
        They tinkled ane by ane.

18 Four and twanty gay gude knichts
        Rade by Fair Annet's side,
    And four and twanty fair ladies,
        As gin she had bin a bride.

19 And whan she cam to Marie's kirk,
        She sat on Marie's stean:
    The cleading that Fair Annet had on
        It skinkled in their een.

20 And whan she cam into the kirk,
        She shimmerd like the sun;
    The belt that was about her waist
        Was a' wi pearles bedone.

21 She sat her by the nut-browne bride,
        And her een they wer sae clear,
    Lord Thomas he clean forgat the bride,
        Whan Fair Annet drew near.

22 He had a rose into his hand,
        He gae it kisses three,
    And reaching by the nut-browne bride,
        Laid it on Fair Annet's knee.

23 Up than spak the nut-brown bride,
        She spak wi meikle spite:
    'And whair gat ye that rose-water,
        That does mak yee sae white?'

17 yae tift *every puff*
19 Marie's kirk *St Mary's Church* · Marie's
stean *stone at or in St Mary's Church* ·
cleading *clothing* · skinkled *sparkled*
20 bedone *ornamented*

24 'O I did get the rose-water
    Whair ye wull neir get nane,
For I did get that very rose-water
    Into my mither's wame.'

25 The bride she drew a long bodkin
    Frae out her gay head-gear,
And strake Fair Annet unto the heart,
    That word spak nevir mair.

26 Lord Thomas he saw Fair Annet wex pale,
    And marvelit what mote bee;
But whan he saw her dear heart's blude,
    A' wood-wroth wexed hee.

27 He drew his dagger, that was sae sharp,
    That was sae sharp and meet,
And drave it into the nut-browne bride,
    That fell deid at his feit.

28 'Now stay for me, dear Annet,' he sed,
    'Now stay, my dear,' he cry'd;
Then strake the dagger untill his heart,
    And fell deid by her side.

29 Lord Thomas was buried without kirk-wa,
    Fair Annet within the quiere,
And o the tane thair grew a birk,
    The other a bonny briere.

30 And ay they grew, and ay they threw,
    As they wad faine be neare;
And by this ye may ken right weil
    They were twa luvers deare.

24 wame *womb* · 25 bodkin *ornamental pin*
26 wex *grow* · mote *might* · wood-wroth *mad
with rage*
29 quiere *choir* · birk *birch*
30 threw *intertwined*

The Twa Sisters

1 There was twa sisters in a bowr,
     Edinburgh, Edinburgh
  There was twa sisters in a bowr,
     Stirling for ay
  There was twa sisters in a bowr,
  There came a knight to be their wooer.
     Bonny Saint Johnston stands upon Tay

2 He courted the eldest wi glove an ring,
  But he lovd the youngest above a' thing.

3 He courted the eldest wi brotch an knife,
  But lovd the youngest as his life.

4 The eldest she was vexed sair,
  An much envi'd her sister fair.

5 Into her bowr she could not rest,
  Wi grief an spite she almos brast.

6 Upon a morning fair an clear,
  She cried upon her sister dear:

7 'O sister, come to yon sea stran,
  An see our father's ships come to lan.'

8 She's taen her by the milk-white han,
  An led her down to yon sea stran.

9 The younges[t] stood upon a stane,
  The eldest came an threw her in.

10 She tooke her by the middle sma,
  An dashd her bonny back to the jaw.

1 Saint Johnston *Perth* · 5 brast *burst*
6 cried upon *called* · 10 jaw *wave*

11 'O sister, sister, tak my han,
      An Ise mack you heir to a' my lan.

12 'O sister, sister, tak my middle,
      An yes get my goud and my gouden girdle.

13 'O sister, sister, save my life,
      An I swear Ise never be nae man's wife.'

14 'Foul fa the han that I should tacke,
      It twin'd me an my wardles make.

15 'Your cherry cheeks an yellow hair
      Gars me gae maiden for evermair.'

16 Sometimes she sank, an sometimes she swam,
      Till she came down yon bonny mill-dam.

17 O out it came the miller's son,
      An saw the fair maid swimmin in.

18 'O father, father, draw your dam,
      Here's either a mermaid or a swan.'

19 The miller quickly drew the dam,
      An there he found a drownd woman.

20 You coudna see her yellow hair
      For gold and pearle that were so rare.

21 You coudna see her middle sma
      For gouden girdle that was sae braw.

22 You coudna see her fingers white,
      For gouden rings that was sae gryte.

14 twin'd *parted* · wardles make *earthly mate*
18 draw *drain*

23 An by there came a harper fine,
    That harped to the king at dine.

24 When he did look that lady upon,
    He sighd and made a heavy moan.

25 He's taen three locks o her yallow hair,
    An wi them strung his harp sae fair.

26 The first tune he did play and sing,
    Was, 'Farewell to my father the king.'

27 The nextin tune that he playd syne,
    Was, 'Farewell to my mother the queen.'

28 The lasten tune that he playd then,
    Was, 'Wae to my sister, fair Ellen.'

23 dine *dinner*

30

Sweet William's Ghost

1 There came a ghost to Margret's door,
       With many a grievous groan,
   And ay he tirled at the pin,
       But answer made she none.

2 'Is that my father Philip,
       Or is 't my brother John?
   Or is 't my true-love, Willy,
       From Scotland new come home?'

3 ''T is not thy father Philip,
     Nor yet thy brother John;
  But 't is thy true-love, Willy,
     From Scotland new come home.

4 'O sweet Margret, O dear Margret,
     I pray thee speak to me;
  Give me my faith and troth, Margret,
     As I gave it to thee.'

5 'Thy faith and troth thou's never get,
     Nor yet will I thee lend,
  Till that thou come within my bower,
     And kiss my cheek and chin.'

6 'If I shoud come within thy bower,
     I am no earthly man;
  And shoud I kiss thy rosy lips,
     Thy days will not be lang.

7 'O sweet Margret, O dear Margret,
     I pray thee speak to me;
  Give me my faith and troth, Margret,
     As I gave it to thee.'

8 'Thy faith and troth thou's never get,
     Nor yet will I thee lend,
  Till you take me to yon kirk,
     And wed me with a ring.'

9 'My bones are buried in yon kirk-yard,
     Afar beyond the sea,
  And it is but my spirit, Margret,
     That's now speaking to thee.'

5 lend *give*

10 She stretchd out her lilly-white hand,
        And, for to do her best,
    'Hae, there's your faith and troth, Willy,
        God send your soul good rest.'

11 Now she has kilted her robes of green
        A piece below her knee,
    And a' the live-lang winter night
        The dead corp followed she.

12 'Is there any room at your head, Willy?
        Or any room at your feet?
    Or any room at your side, Willy,
        Wherein that I may creep?'

13 'There's no room at my head, Margret,
        There's no room at my feet;
    There's no room at my side, Margret,
        My coffin's made so meet.'

14 Then up and crew the red, red cock,
        And up then crew the gray:
    'Tis time, tis time, my dear Margret,
        That you were going away.'

15 No more the ghost to Margret said,
        But, with a grievous groan,
    Evanishd in a cloud of mist,
        And left her all alone.

16 'O stay, my only true-love, stay,'
        The constant Margret cry'd;
    Wan grew her cheeks, she closd her een,
        Stretchd her soft limbs, and dy'd.

11 kilted *tucked* · piece *little* · 13 meet *good a fit*

31

The Wife of Usher's Well

1 There lived a wife at Usher's Well,
    And a wealthy wife was she;
She had three stout and stalwart sons,
    And sent them oer the sea.

2 They hadna been a week from her,
    A week but barely ane,
Whan word came to the carline wife
    That her three sons were gane.

3 They hadna been a week from her,
    A week but barely three,
Whan word came to the carlin wife
    That her sons she'd never see.

4 'I wish the wind may never cease,
    Nor fashes in the flood,
Till my three sons come hame to me,
    In earthly flesh and blood.'

5 It fell about the Martinmass,
    When nights are lang and mirk,
The carlin wife's three sons came hame,
    And their hats were o the birk.

6 It neither grew in syke nor ditch,
    Nor yet in ony sheugh;
But at the gates o Paradise,
    That birk grew fair eneugh.

* * * * *

2 carline wife *old woman*
4 fashes *troubles, disturbances* · flood *sea*
5 birk *birch*
6 syke *trench* · sheugh *furrow*

7 'Blow up the fire, my maidens,
    Bring water from the well;
For a' my house shall feast this night,
    Since my three sons are well.'

8 And she has made to them a bed,
    She's made it large and wide,
And she's taen her mantle her about,
    Sat down at the bed-side.

★ ★ ★ ★ ★

9 Up then crew the red, red cock,
    And up the crew the gray;
The eldest to the youngest said,
    'T is time we were away.

10 The cock he hadna crawd but once,
    And clappd his wings at a',
When the youngest to the eldest said,
    Brother, we must awa.

11 'The cock doth craw, the day doth daw,
    The channerin worm doth chide;
Gin we be mist out o our place,
    A sair pain we maun bide.

12 'Fare ye weel, my mother dear!
    Fareweel to barn and byre!
And fare ye weel, the bonny lass
    That kindles my mother's fire!'

11 daw *dawn* · channerin *grumbling*

[119]

32

The Maid of Coldingham

1 The may's to the well to wash & to wring
    The primrose o' the wood wants a name
  An' ay so sweetly did she sing
    I am the fair maid of Coldingham

2 O by there cam' an eldren man
    The primrose o' the wood wants a name
  O gie me a drink o' your cauld stream
    An' ye be the fair maiden of Coldingham

3 My golden cup is down the strand
    The primrose, etc.
  Of my cold water ye sall drink nane
    Tho' I be the fair maiden, etc.

4 O fair may bethink ye again
    The primrose, etc.
  Gie a drink o' cauld water to an auld man
    If ye be the fair, etc.

5 O she sware by the sun & the moon
    The primrose, etc.
  That all her cups were flown to Rome
    Yet she was the fair maid of, etc.

6 O seven bairns hae ye born
    The primrose, etc.
  An' as many lives hae ye forlorn
    An' ye're nae the fair maiden, etc.

7 There's three o' them in your bower floor
    The primrose, etc.
  It gars ye fear when ye woudna fear
    An' ye're nae the fair maiden, etc.

1 may *maid* · wants *lacks* · 2 eldren *old* · 3 strand *stream*
4 bethink ye *consider* · 6 forlorn *destroyed*

8   There's ane o' them in yon well stripe
        The primrose, etc.
    An' twa o' them in the garden dyke
        An' yere nae the fair maiden, etc.

9   There's ane o' them in your bed feet
        The primrose, etc.
    It gars you wake when ye should sleep
        An' yere nae the fair, etc.

10 Ye'll be seven year a cocky to craw
        The primrose, etc.
    An' seven years a cattie to maiw
        An' ye're nae the fair maiden, etc.

11 Ye'll be seven lang years a stane in a cairn
        The primrose, etc.
    An' seven years ye'll go wi' bairn
        An' ye're nae the fair maiden of Coldingham

12 Ye'll be seven years a sacran bell
        The primrose, etc.
    An' ither seven the cook in hell
        An' ye're nae the fair, etc.

8 dyke *wall* · stripe *stream*
12 sacran bell *bell used in church services*

33

Clark Colven

1   Clark Colven and his gay ladie,
      As they walked to yon garden green,
  A belt about her middle gimp,
      Which cost Clark Colven crowns fifteen:

2   'O hearken weel now, my good lord,
      O hearken weel to what I say;
  When ye gang to the wall o Stream,
      O gang nae neer the well-fared may.'

3   'O haud your tongue, my gay ladie,
      Tak nae sic care o me;
  For I nae saw a fair woman
      I like so well as thee.'

4   He mounted on his berry-brown steed,
      And merry, merry rade he on,
  Till he came to the wall o Stream,
      And there he saw the mermaiden.

5   'Ye wash, ye wash, ye bonny may,
      And ay's ye wash your sark o silk:'
  'It's a' for you, ye gentle knight,
      My skin is whiter than the milk.'

6   He's taen her by the milk-white hand,
      He's taen her by the sleeve sae green,
  And he's forgotten his gay ladie,
      And away with the fair maiden.

* * * * *

1 gimp *slender* · 2 well-fared may *attractive maid*
5 sark *shift*

7 'Ohon, alas!' says Clark Colven,
      'And aye sae sair's I mean my head!'
  And merrily leugh the mermaiden,
      'O win on till you be dead.

8 'But out ye tak your little pen-knife,
      And frae my sark ye shear a gare;
  Row that about your lovely head,
      And the pain ye'll never feel nae mair.'

9 Out he has taen his little pen-knife,
      And frae her sark he's shorn a gare,
  Rowed that about his lovely head,
      But the pain increased mair and mair.

10 'Ohon, alas!' says Clark Colven,
       'An aye sae sair's I mean my head!'
   And merrily laughd the mermaiden,
       'It will ay be war till ye be dead.'

11 Then out he drew his trusty blade,
       And thought wi it to be her dead,
   But she's become a fish again,
       And merrily sprang into the fleed.

12 He's mounted on his berry-brown steed,
       And dowy, dowy rade he home,
   And heavily, heavily lighted down
       When to his ladie's bower-door he came.

13 'Oh, mither, mither, mak my bed,
       And, gentle ladie, lay me down;
   Oh, brither, brither, unbend my bow,
       'T will never be bent by me again.'

7 mean my head *lament the state of my head* ·
leugh *laughed* · win on *keep on*
8 shear *cut* · gare *strip* · row *wind* · 10 war *worse*
11 dead *death* · 12 dowy *sad* · 13 unbend *unstring*

14 His mither she has made his bed,
        His gentle ladie laid him down,
    His brither he has unbent his bow,
        'T was never bent by him again.

34

The Great Silkie of Sule Skerry

1 An eartly nourris sits and sings,
        And aye she sings, Ba, lily wean!
    Little ken I my bairnis father,
        Far less the land that he staps in.

2 Then ane arose at her bed-fit,
        An a grumly guest I'm sure was he:
    'Here am I, thy bairnis father,
        Although that I be not comelie.

3 'I am a man, upo the lan,
        An I am a silkie in the sea;
    And when I'm far and far frae lan,
        My dwelling is in Sule Skerrie.'

4 'It was na weel,' quo the maiden fair,
        'It was na weel, indeed,' quo she,
    'That the Great Silkie of Sule Skerrie
        Suld hae come and aught a bairn to me.'

5 Now he has taen a purse of goud,
        And he has pat it upo her knee,
    Sayin, Gie to me my little young son,
        An tak thee up thy nourris-fee.

TITLE silkie *seal*
1 nourris *nurse* · ba, lily wean *hush, lovely child* · staps *lives*
2 grumly *fierce-looking*
4 aught a bairn to me *had a child by me*

[124]

6 An it sall come to pass on a simmer's day,
    When the sin shines het on evera stane,
That I will tak my little young son,
    An teach him for to swim the faem.

7 An thu sall marry a proud gunner,
    An a proud gunner I'm sure he'll be,
An the very first schot that ere he schoots,
    He'll schoot baith my young son and me.

35

Tam Lin

1 O I forbid you, maidens a',
    That wear gowd on your hair,
To come or gae by Carterhaugh,
    For young Tam Lin is there.

2 There's nane that gaes by Carterhaugh
    But they leave him a wad,
Either their rings, or green mantles,
    Or else their maidenhead.

3 Janet has kilted her green kirtle
    A little aboon her knee,
And she has broded her yellow hair
    A little aboon her bree,
And she's awa to Carterhaugh,
    As fast as she can hie.

4 When she came to Carterhaugh
    Tam Lin was at the well,
And there she fand his steed standing,
    But away was himsel.

2 wad *forfeit* · 3 kilted *tucked up* · kirtle *petticoat*

5 She had na pu'd a double rose,
      A rose but only twa,
   Till up then started young Tam Lin,
      Says, Lady, thou's pu nae mae.

6 Why pu's thou the rose, Janet,
      And why breaks thou the wand?
   Or why comes thou to Carterhaugh
      Withoutten my command?

7 'Carterhaugh, it is my ain,
      My daddie gave it me;
   I'll come and gang by Carterhaugh,
      And ask nae leave at thee.'

                    * * * * *

8 Janet has kilted her green kirtle
      A little aboon her knee,
   And she has snooded her yellow hair
      A little aboon her bree,
   And she is to her father's ha,
      As fast as she can hie.

9 Four and twenty ladies fair
      Were playing at the ba,
   And out then cam the fair Janet,
      Ance the flower amang them a'.

10 Four and twenty ladies fair
      Were playing at the chess,
   And out then cam the fair Janet,
      As green as onie glass.

8 snooded *tied up with a fillet*

11 Out then spak an auld grey knight,
        Lay oer the castle wa,
    And says, Alas, fair Janet, for thee
        But we'll be blamed a'.

12 'Haud your tongue, ye auld fac'd knight,
        Some ill death may ye die!
    Father my bairn on whom I will,
        I'll father nane on thee.'

13 Out then spak her father dear,
        And he spak meek and mild;
    'And ever alas, sweet Janet,' he says,
        'I think thou gaes wi child.'

14 'If that I gae wi child, father,
        Mysel maun bear the blame;
    There's neer a laird about your ha
        Shall get the bairn's name.

15 'If my love were an earthly knight,
        As he's an elfin grey,
    I wad na gie my ain true-love
        For nae lord that ye hae.

16 'The steed that my true-love rides on
        Is lighter than the wind;
    Wi siller he is shod before,
        Wi burning gowd behind.'

17 Janet has kilted her green kirtle
        A little aboon her knee,
    And she has snooded her yellow hair
        A little aboon her bree,
    And she's awa to Carterhaugh,
        As fast as she can hie.

18 When she cam to Carterhaugh,
    Tam Lin was at the well,
And there she fand his steed standing,
    But away was himsel.

19 She had na pu'd a double rose,
    A rose but only twa,
Till up then started young Tam Lin,
    Says Lady, thou pu's nae mae.

20 Why pu's thou the rose, Janet,
    Amang the groves sae green,
And a' to kill the bonie babe
    That we gat us between?

21 'O tell me, tell me, Tam Lin,' she says,
    'For's sake that died on tree,
If eer ye was in holy chapel,
    Or christendom did see?'

22 'Roxbrugh he was my grandfather,
    Took me with him to bide,
And ance it fell upon a day
    That wae did me betide.

23 'And ance it fell upon a day,
    A cauld day and a snell,
When we were frae the hunting come,
    That frae my horse I fell;
The Queen o Fairies she caught me,
    In yon green hill to dwell.

21 for's sake that died on tree *for the sake
of him who died on the cross*
23 snell *bitter*

24 'And pleasant is the fairy land,
But, an eerie tale to tell,
Ay at the end of seven years
We pay a tiend to hell;
I am sae fair and fu o flesh,
I'm feard it be mysel.

25 'But the night is Halloween, lady,
The morn is Hallowday;
Then win me, win me, an ye will,
For weel I wat ye may.

26 'Just at the mirk and midnight hour
The fairy folk will ride,
And they that wad their true-love win,
At Miles Cross they maun bide.'

27 'But how shall I thee ken, Tam Lin,
Or how my true-love know,
Amang sae mony unco knights
The like I never saw?'

28 'O first let pass the black, lady,
And syne let pass the brown,
But quickly run to the milk-white steed,
Pu ye his rider down.

29 'For I'll ride on the milk-white steed,
And ay nearest the town;
Because I was an earthly knight
They gie me that renown.

24 eerie tale *tale full of dread* · tiend *tithe* ·
feard *afraid*
25 the night *tonight* · the morn *tomorrow*
27 unco *strange*

30 'My right hand will be glovd, lady,
 My left hand will be bare,
Cockt up shall my bonnet be,
 And kaimd down shall my hair,
And thae's the takens I gie thee,
 Nae doubt I will be there.

31 'They'll turn me in your arms, lady,
 Into an esk and adder;
But hold me fast, and fear me not,
 I am your bairn's father.

32 'They'll turn me to a bear sae grim,
 And then a lion bold;
But hold me fast, and fear me not,
 As ye shall love your child.

33 'Again they'll turn me in your arms
 To a red het gaud of airn;
But hold me fast, and fear me not,
 I'll do to you nae harm.

34 'And last they'll turn me in your arms
 Into the burning gleed;
Then throw me into well water,
 O throw me in wi speed.

35 'And then I'll be your ain true-love,
 I'll turn a naked knight;
Then cover me wi your green mantle,
 And cover me out o sight.'

30 thae 's *these are* · 31 esk *newt*
33 gaud of airn *iron bar*
34 gleed *ember*

36 Gloomy, gloomy was the night,
  And eerie was the way,
As fair Jenny in her green mantle
  To Miles Cross she did gae.

37 About the middle o the night
  She heard the bridles ring;
This lady was as glad at that
  As any earthly thing.

38 First she let the black pass by,
  And syne she let the brown;
But quickly she ran to the milk-white steed,
  And pu'd the rider down.

39 Sae weel she minded what he did say,
  And young Tam Lin did win;
Syne coverd him wi her green mantle,
  As blythe's a bird in spring.

40 Out then spak the Queen o Fairies,
  Out of a bush o broom:
'Them that has gotten young Tam Lin
  Has gotten a stately groom.'

41 Out then spak the Queen o Fairies,
  And an angry woman was she:
'Shame betide her ill-far'd face,
  And an ill death may she die,
For she's taen awa the boniest knight
  In a' my companie.

42 'But had I kend, Tam Lin,' she says,
  'What now this night I see,
I wad hae taen out thy twa grey een,
  And put in twa een o tree.'

36 eerie *arousing dread of the supernatural*
39 minded *heeded* · 41 ill-far'd *ugly* · 42 tree *wood*

Thomas the Rhymer

1 True Thomas lay on Huntlie bank,
    A ferlie he spied wi' his ee,
And there he saw a lady bright,
    Come riding down by the Eildon Tree.

2 Her shirt was o the grass-green silk,
    Her mantle o the velvet fyne,
At ilka tett of her horse's mane
    Hang fifty siller bells and nine.

3 True Thomas, he pulld aff his cap,
    And louted low down to his knee:
'All hail, thou mighty Queen of Heaven!
    For thy peer on earth I never did see.'

4 'O no, O no, Thomas,' she said,
    'That name does not belang to me;
I am but the queen of fair Elfland,
    That am hither come to visit thee.

5 'Harp and carp, Thomas,' she said,
    'Harp and carp along wi me,
And if ye dare to kiss my lips,
    Sure of your bodie I will be.'

6 'Betide me weal, betide me woe,
    That weird shall never daunton me;'
Syne he has kissed her rosy lips,
    All underneath the Eildon Tree.

1 ferlie *marvel* · bright *beautiful*
2 ilka tett *each lock*
3 louted *bent*
5 harp and carp *play the harp and sing*
6 weird *fate* · daunton *intimidate*

7 'Now, ye maun go wi me,' she said,
        'True Thomas, ye maun go wi me,
And ye maun serve me seven years,
        Thro weal or woe, as may chance to be.'

8 She mounted on her milk-white steed,
        She's taen True Thomas up behind,
And aye wheneer her bridle rung,
        The steed flew swifter than the wind.

9 O they rade on, and farther on —
        The steed gaed swifter than the wind —
Untill they reached a desart wide,
        And living land was left behind.

10 'Light down, light down, now, True Thomas,
        And lean your head upon my knee;
Abide and rest a little space,
        And I will shew you ferlies three.

11 'O see ye not yon narrow road,
        So thick beset with thorns and briers?
That is the path of righteousness,
        Tho after it but few enquires.

12 'And see not ye that braid braid road,
        That lies across that lily leven?
That is the path of wickedness,
        Tho some call it the road to heaven.

13 'And see not ye that bonny road,
        That winds about the fernie brae?
That is the road to fair Elfland,
        Where thou and I this night maun gae.

12 lily leven *fair plain*
13 fernie brae *fern-covered hillside*

14 'But, Thomas, ye maun hold your tongue,
　　　Whatever ye may hear or see,
For, if you speak word in Elflyn land,
　　　Ye'll neer get back to your ain countrie.'

15 O they rade on, and farther on,
　　　And they waded thro rivers aboon the knee,
And they saw neither sun nor moon,
　　　But they heard the roaring of the sea.

16 It was mirk mirk night, and there was nae stern light,
　　　And they waded thro red blude to the knee;
For a' the blude that's shed on earth
　　　Rins thro the springs o that countrie.

17 Syne they came on to a garden green,
　　　And she pu'd an apple frae a tree:
'Take this for thy wages, True Thomas,
　　　It will give thee the tongue that can never lie.'

18 'My tongue is mine ain,' True Thomas said;
　　　'A gudely gift ye wad gie to me!
I neither dought to buy nor sell,
　　　At fair or tryst where I may be.

19 'I dought neither speak to prince or peer,
　　　Nor ask of grace from fair ladye:'
'Now hold thy peace,' the lady said,
　　　'For as I say, so must it be.'

20 He has gotten a coat of the even cloth,
　　　And a pair of shoes of velvet green,
And till seven years were gane and past
　　　True Thomas on earth was never seen.

16 stern *star* · 18 dought *could* · tryst *market*
20 even *smooth*

37

King Orpheus

1 There lived a Lady in yon Haa,
    Scowan Orlaa Grona;
Her name was Lady Lisa Bell,
    Where gurtin grew for Norla.

2 One day the King a hunting went,
They wounded the Lady to the heart.

3 The King of the Fairies we his dart,
Wounded his Lady to the heart.

4 So when the King came home at noon,
He asked for Lady Lisa Bell.

5 His nobles unto him did say,
My Lady was wounded, but now she is dead.

6 Now they have taen her life fra me,
But her corps they's never ha.

7 Now he have called his nobles aa,
To waltz her corps into the Haa.

8 But when the Lords was faen asleep,
Her corps out of the house did sweep.

9 Now he's awa' to the wood, wood were,
And there he's to sit till grown o'er we hair.

10 He had not sitten seven long years,
Till a company to him drew near.

7 waltz *wake, watch* · into *in*
9 wood, wood were *wilderness* (exact sense not clear)

11 Some did ride and some did ging,
     He saw his Lady them among.

12 There stood a Haa upon yon hill,
     There went aa the Ladie's tilt.

13 He is laid him on his belly to swim,
     When he came it was a gray stane.

14 Now he's set him down ful wae,
     And he's taen out his pipes to play.

15 First he played the notes of noy,
     Then he played the notes of joy.

16 And then he played the gaber reel,
     That might a made a sick heart heal.

17 There came a boy out of the Haa,
     Ye'r bidden to come in among us aa.

18 The formost man to him did say,
     What thou' ha' for thy play.

19 For my play I will thee tell,
     I'll ha' my Lady Lisa Bell.

20 Thy sister's son, that unworthy thing,
     To-morrow as to be crowned King.

21 But thou's take her and thou's go hem,
     And thou shalt be King o'er thy own.

11 ging *walk* · 15 noy *grief*
16 gaber reel *sprightly dance music*

38

Sir Colin

1 The king luikit owre his castle wa,
      To his nobles ane an a';
  Says, Whare it is him Sir Colin,
      I dinna see him amang you a'?

2 Up it spak an eldern knicht,
      Aye an even up spak he:
  'Sir Colin's sick for your dochter Janet,
      He's very sick, an like to dee.'

3 'Win up, win up, my dochter Janet,
      I wat ye are a match most fine;
  Tak the baken bread an wine sae ried,
      An to Sir Colin ye maun gieng.'

4 Up she rase, that fair Janet,
      An I wat weel she was na sweer,
  An up they rase, her merrie maries,
      An they said a' they wad gae wi her.

5 'No, no,' said fair Janet,
      'No, no such thing can be;
  For a thrang to gae to a sick man's bour,
      I think it wald be great folie.

6 'How is my knicht, all last nicht?'
      'Very sick an like to dee;
  But if I had a kiss o your sweet lips,
      I wald lie nae langer here.'

2 eldern *old* · even up *bluntly*
3 win up *get up*
4 sweer *reluctant* · maries *maids-in-waiting*
5 thrang *crowd*

7 She leant her doon on his bed-side,
      I wat she gae him kisses three;
   But wi sighen said that fair Janet,
      'As for your bride, I daurna be.

8 'Unless you watch the Orlange hill,
      An at that hill there grows a thorn;
   There neer cam a liven man frae it,
      Sin the first nicht that I was born.'

9 'Oh I will watch the Orlange hill,
      Though I waur thinkin to be slain;
   But I will gie you some love tokens,
      In case we never meet again.'

10 He gae her rings to her fingers,
       Sae did he ribbons to her hair;
    He gae her a broach to her briest-bane,
       For fear that they sud neer meet mair.

11 She put her hand in her pocket,
       An she took out a lang, lang wand;
    'As lang 's ony man this wand sall keep,
       There sall not a drap o his blude be drawn.'

12 Whan een was come, an een-bells rung,
       An a' man boun for bed,
    There beheld him Sir Colin,
       Fast to the Orlange hill he rade.

13 The wind blew trees oot at the rutes,
       Sae did it auld castles doon;
    'T was eneuch to fricht ony Christian knicht,
       To be sae far frae ony toon.

12 een *evening* · boun *ready*
13 toon *habitation*

[138]

14 He rade up, sae did he doon,
    He rade even through the loan,
Till he spied a knicht, wi a ladie bricht,
    Wi a bent bow intil his han.

15 She cried afar, ere she cam naur,
    I warn ye, kind sir, I rede ye flee;
That for the love you bear to me,
    I warn ye, kind sir, that ye flee.

16 They faucht up, sae did they doon,
    They faucht even through the loan,
Till he cut aff the king's richt han,
    Was set aboot wi chains a' goud.

17 'Haud your hand now, Sir Colin,
    I wat you've dung my love richt sair;
Noo for the love ye bear to me,
    See that ye ding my love nae mair.'

18 He wooed, he wooed that fair Janet,
    He wooed her and he brocht her hame;
He wooed, he wooed that fair Janet,
    An ca'd her Dear-Coft till her name.

14 loan *common* · 15 rede *advise*
17 dung *struck* · ding *strike*
18 Dear-Coft *Dear-Bought*

39

The Twa Magicians

1   The lady stands in her bower door,
    As straight as willow wand;
The blacksmith stood a little forebye,
    Wi hammer in his hand.

2   'Weel may ye dress ye, lady fair,
    Into your robes o red;
Before the morn at this same time,
    I'll gain your maidenhead.'

3   'Awa, awa, ye coal-black smith,
    Woud ye do me the wrang
To think to gain my maidenhead,
    That I hae kept sae lang!'

4   Then she has hadden up her hand,
    And she sware by the mold,
'I wudna be a blacksmith's wife
    For the full o a chest o gold.

5   'I'd rather I were dead and gone,
    And my body laid in grave,
Ere a rusty stock o coal-black smith
    My maidenhead shoud have.'

6   But he has hadden up his hand,
    And he sware by the mass,
'I'll cause ye be my light leman
    For the hauf o that and less.'
        O bide, lady, bide,
            And aye he bade her bide;
        The rusty smith your leman shall be,
            For a' your muckle pride.

1 a little forebye *near by* · 4 mold *earth*
5 stock *block* · 6 light leman *whore*

7 Then she became a turtle dow,
      To fly up in the air,
And he became another dow,
      And they flew pair and pair.
        O bide, lady, bide, &c.

8 She turnd hersell into an eel,
      To swim into yon burn,
And he became a speckled trout,
      To gie the eel a turn.
        O bide, lady, bide, &c.

9 Then she became a duck, a duck,
      To puddle in a peel,
And he became a rose-kaimd drake,
      To gie the duck a dreel.
        O bide, lady, bide, &c.

10 She turnd hersell into a hare,
      To rin upon yon hill,
And he became a gude grey-hound,
      And boldly he did fill.
        O bide, lady, bide, &c.

11 Then she became a gay grey mare,
      And stood in yonder slack,
And he became a gilt saddle,
      And sat upon her back.
        Was she wae, he held her sae,
          And still he bade her bide;
        The rusty smith her leman was,
          For a' her muckle pride.

7 dow *dove* · 10 fill *follow*
11 slack *low ground*

12 Then she became a het girdle,
     And he became a cake,
   And a' the ways she turnd hersell,
     The blacksmith was her make.
       Was she wae, &c.

13 She turnd hersell into a ship,
     To sail out ower the flood;
   He ca'ed a nail intill her tail,
     And syne the ship she stood.
       Was she wae, &c.

14 Then she became a silken plaid,
     And stretchd upon a bed,
   And he became a green covering,
     And gaind her maidenhead.
       Was she wae, &c.

12 girdle *griddle* · make *mate*
13 ca'ed *drove*

40

The Broomfield Hill

1 There was a knight and a lady bright,
     Had a true tryste at the broom;
   The ane gaed early in the morning,
     The other in the afternoon.

2 And ay she sat in her mother's bower door,
     And ay she made her mane:
   'O whether should I gang to the Broomfield Hill,
     Or should I stay at hame?

1 bright *beautiful* · tryste *appointment to meet*
2 made her mane *said*

3 'For if I gang to the Broomfield Hill,
    My maidenhead is gone;
And if I chance to stay at hame,
    My love will ca me mansworn.'

4 Up then spake a witch-woman,
    Ay from the room aboon:
'O ye may gang to the Broomfield Hill,
    And yet come maiden hame.

5 'For when ye gang to the Broomfield Hill,
    Ye'll find your love asleep,
With a silver belt about his head,
    And a broom-cow at his feet.

6 'Take ye the blossom of the broom,
    The blossom it smells sweet,
And strew it at your true-love's head,
    And likewise at his feet.

7 'Take ye the rings off your fingers,
    Put them on his right hand,
To let him know, when he doth awake,
    His love was at his command.'

8 She pu'd the broom flower on Hive Hill,
    And strewd on 's white hals-bane,
And that was to be wittering true
    That maiden she had gane.

9 'O where were ye, my milk-white steed,
    That I hae coft sae dear,
That wadna watch and waken me
    When there was maiden here?'

3 mansworn *perjured*
5 broom-cow *twig of broom*
8 hals-bane *collar bone* · wittering *token*
9 coft *bought*

10 'I stamped wi my foot, master,
    And gard my bridle ring,
But na kin thing wald waken ye,
    Till she was past and gane.'

11 'And wae betide ye, my gay goss-hawk,
    That I did love sae dear,
That wadna watch and waken me
    When there was maiden here.'

12 'I clapped wi my wings, master,
    And aye my bells I rang,
And aye cry'd, Waken, waken, master,
    Before the ladye gang.'

13 'But haste and haste, my gude white steed,
    To come the maiden till,
Or a' the birds of gude green wood
    Of your flesh shall have their fill.'

14 'Ye need na burst your gude white steed
    Wi racing oer the howm;
Nae bird flies faster through the wood,
    Than she fled through the broom.'

10 na kin thing *no kind of thing, nothing*
14 howm *flat ground by a river*

41

Gil Brenton

1 Gil Brenton has sent oer the fame,
  He's woo'd a wife an brought her hame.

2 Full sevenscore o ships came her wi,
  The lady by the greenwood tree.

3 There was twal an twal wi beer an wine,
An twal an twal wi muskadine:

4 An twall an twall wi bouted flowr,
An twall an twall wi paramour:

5 An twall an twall wi baken bread,
An twall an twall wi the goud sae red.

6 Sweet Willy was a widow's son,
An at her stirrup-foot he did run.

7 An she was dressd i the finest pa,
But ay she loot the tears down fa.

8 An she was deckd wi the fairest flowrs,
But ay she loot the tears down pour.

9 'O is there water i your shee?
Or does the win blaw i your glee?

10 'Or are you mourning i your meed
That eer you left your mither gueede?

11 'Or are ye mourning i your tide
That ever ye was Gil Brenton's bride?'

12 'The[re] is nae water i my shee,
Nor does the win blaw i my glee:

13 'Nor am I mourning i my tide
That eer I was Gil Brenton's bride:

3 twal *twelve* · muskadine *muscatel, a strong,*
sweet wine
4 bouted flowr *sifted flour* · paramour *usually*
lover but meaningless in this context
7 pa *fine cloth* · 9 glee *glove*
10 meed *mood* · 11 tide *time*

[145]

14 'But I am mourning i my meed
    That ever I left my mither gueede.

15 'But, bonny boy, tell to me
    What is the customs o your country.'

16 'The customs o't, my dame,' he says,
    'Will ill a gentle lady please.

17 'Seven king's daughters has our king wedded,
    An seven king's daughters has our king bedded.

18 'But he's cutted the paps frae their breast-bane,
    An sent them mourning hame again.

19 'But whan you come to the palace yate,
    His mither a golden chair will set.

20 'An be you maid or be you nane,
    O sit you there till the day be dane.

21 'An gin you're sure that you are a maid,
    Ye may gang safely to his bed.

22 'But gin o that you be na sure,
    Then hire some woman o youre bowr.'

23 O whan she came to the palace yate,
    His mither a golden chair did set.

24 An was she maid or was she nane,
    She sat in it till the day was dane.

25 An she's calld on her bowr woman,
    That waiting was her bowr within.

26 'Five hundred pound, maid, I'll gi to the,
    An sleep this night wi the king for me.'

27 Whan bells was rung, an mass was sung,
   An a' man unto bed was gone,

28 Gil Brenton an the bonny maid
   Intill ae chamber they were laid.

29 'O speak to me, blankets, an speak to me, sheets,
   An speak to me, cods, that under me sleeps;

30 'Is this a maid that I ha wedded?
   Is this a maid that I ha bedded?'

31 'It's nae a maid that you ha wedded,
   But it's a maid that you ha bedded.

32 'Your lady's in her bigly bowr,
   An for you she drees mony sharp showr.'

33 O he has taen him thro the ha,
   And on his mither he did ca.

34 'I am the most unhappy man
   That ever was in christend lan.

35 'I woo'd a maiden meek an mild,
   An I've marryed a woman great wi child.'

36 'O stay, my son, intill this ha,
   An sport you wi your merry men a'.

37 'An I'll gang to yon painted bowr,
   An see how't fares wi yon base whore.'

38 The auld queen she was stark an strang;
   She gard the door flee aff the ban.

29 cods *pillows*
32 bigly *pleasant* · drees *suffers* · showr *pain*
38 stark *powerful* · ban *hinge*

39   The auld queen she was stark an steer;
     She gard the door lye i the fleer.

40   'O is your bairn to laird or loon?
     Or is it to your father's groom?'

41   'My bairn's na to laird or loon,
     Nor is it to my father's groom.

42   'But hear me, mither, on my knee,
     An my hard wierd I'll tell to thee.

43   'O we were sisters, sisters seven,
     We was the fairest under heaven.

44   'We had nae mair for our seven years wark
     But to shape an sue the king's son a sark.

45   'O it fell on a Saturday's afternoon,
     Whan a' our langsome wark was dane,

46   'We keist the cavils us amang,
     To see which shoud to the greenwood gang.

47   'Ohone, alas! for I was youngest,
     An ay my wierd it was the hardest.

48   'The cavil it did on me fa,
     Which was the cause of a' my wae.

49   'For to the greenwood I must gae,
     To pu the nut but an the slae;

39 steer *sturdy*
40 loon *man of low rank*
42 wierd *fortune*
44 shape an sue *cut out and sow* · sark *shirt*
45 langsome *wearisome*
46 keist the cavils *cast lots*
49 but an the slae *and also the sloe*

50 'To pu the red rose an the thyme,
   To strew my mother's bowr and mine.

51 'I had na pu'd a flowr but ane,
   Till by there came a jelly hind greeme,

52 'Wi high-colld hose an laigh-colld shoone,
   An he 'peard to be some kingis son.

53 'An be I maid or be I nane,
   He kept me there till the day was dane.

54 'An be I maid or be I nae,
   He kept me there till the close of day.

55 'He gae me a lock of yallow hair,
   An bade me keep it for ever mair.

56 'He gae me a carket o gude black beads,
   An bade me keep them against my needs.

57 'He gae to me a gay gold ring,
   An bade me ke[e]p it aboon a' thing.

58 'He gae to me a little pen-kniffe,
   An bade me keep it as my life.'

59 'What did you wi these tokens rare
   That ye got frae that young man there?'

60 'O bring that coffer hear to me,
   And a' the tokens ye sal see.'

51 jelly hind greeme *handsome, courteous man*
52 high-colld *long* · laigh-colld *low-cut*
56 carket *necklace*
57 a' thing *everything* · 60 coffer *box*

61 An ay she ranked, an ay she flang,
   Till a' the tokens came till her han.

62 'O stay here, daughter, your bowr within,
   Till I gae parley wi my son.'

63 O she has taen her thro the ha,
   An on her son began to ca.

64 'What did you wi that gay gold ring
   I bade you keep aboon a' thing?

65 'What did you wi that little pen-kniffe
   I bade you keep while you had life?

66 'What did you wi that yallow hair
   I bade you keep for ever mair?

67 'What did you wi that good black beeds
   I bade you keep against your needs?'

68 'I gae them to a lady gay
   I met i the greenwood on a day.

69 'An I would gi a' my father's lan,
   I had that lady my yates within.

70 'I would gi a' my ha's an towrs,
   I had that bright burd i my bowrs.'

71 'O son, keep still your father's lan;
   You hae that lady your yates within.

72 'An keep you still your ha's an towrs;
   You hae that bright burd i your bowrs.'

61 ranked *raged* · flang *flung herself about*
62 parley *speak*
70 bright burd *beautiful lady*

73 Now or a month was come an gone,
   This lady bare a bonny young son.

74 An it was well written on his breast-bane
   'Gil Brenton is my father's name.'

   73 or *before*

42

The Broom of Cowdenknows

1 O the broom, and the bonny, bonny broom,
      And the broom of the Cowdenknows!
   And aye sae sweet as the lassie sang,
      I the bought, milking the ewes.

2 The hills were high on ilka side,
      An the bought i the lirk o the hill,
   And aye, as she sang, her voice it rang
      Out-oer the head o yon hill.

3 There was a troop o gentlemen
      Came riding merrilie by,
   And one o them has rode out o the way,
      To the bought to the bonny may.

4 'Weel may ye save an see, bonny lass,
      An weel may ye save an see!'
   'An sae wi you, ye weel-bred knight,
      And what's your will wi me?'

   1 bought *fold* · 2 ilka *each* · lirk *hollow*
   3 may *young woman*
   4 weel may ye save an see *may God see and protect you*

[151]

5 'The night is misty and mirk, fair may,
   And I have ridden astray,
 And will ye be so kind, fair may,
   As come out and point my way?'

6 'Ride out, ride out, ye ramp rider!
   Your steed's baith stout and strang;
 For out of the bought I dare na come,
   For fear at ye do me wrang.'

7 'O winna ye pity me, bonny lass?
   O winna ye pity me?
 An winna ye pity my poor steed,
   Strands trembling at yon tree?'

8 'I wadna pity your poor steed,
   Tho it were tied to a thorn;
 For if ye wad gain my love the night
   Ye wad ṣlight me ere the morn.

9 'For I ken you by your weel-busked hat,
   And your merrie twinkling ee,
 That ye're the laird o the Oakland hills,
   An ye may weel seem for to be.'

10 'But I am not the laird o the Oakland hills,
   Ye're far mistaen o me;
 But I'm ane o the men about his house,
   An right aft in his companie.'

11 He's taen her by the middle jimp,
   And by the grass-green sleeve,
 He's lifted her over the fauld-dyke,
   And speerd at her sma leave.

6 ramp *wild* · at ye do *that you do*
9 weel-busked *handsomely decorated*
11 jimp *slender* · fauld-dyke *fold wall* · speerd *asked*

12 O he's taen out a purse o gowd,
      And streekd her yellow hair:
    'Now take ye that, my bonnie may,
      Of me till you hear mair.'

13 O he's leapt on his berry-brown steed,
      An soon he's oertaen his men;
    And ane and a' cried out to him,
      O master, ye've tarryd lang!

14 'O I hae been east, and I hae been west,
      An I hae been far oer the knows,
    But the bonniest lass that ever I saw
      Is i the bought, milkin the ewes.'

15 She set the cog upon her head,
      An she's gane singing hame:
    'O where hae ye been, my ae daughter?
      Ye hae na been your lane.'

16 'O nae body was wi me, father,
      O nae body has been wi me;
    The night is misty and mirk, father,
      Ye may gang to the door and see.

17 'But wae be to your ewe-herd, father,
      And an ill deed may he die!
    He bug the bought at the back o the know
      And a tod has frighted me.

18 'There came a tod to the bought-door,
      The like I never saw;
    And ere he had taken the lamb he did
      I had lourd he had taen them a'.'

12 streekd *stroked*
14 knows *hillocks*
15 cog *milk container* · your lane *alone*
17 deed *death* · bug *built* · tod *fox*
18 lourd *rather*

19 O whan fifteen weeks was come and gane,
          Fifteen weeks and three,
    That lassie began to look thin and pale,
          An to long for his merry-twinkling ee.

20 It fell on a day, on a het simmer day,
          She was ca'ing out her father's kye,
    By came a troop o gentlemen,
          A' merrilie riding bye.

21 'Weel may ye save an see, bonny may!
          Weel may ye save and see!
    Weel I wat ye be a very bonny may,
          But whae's aught that babe ye are wi?'

22 Never a word could that lassie say,
          For never a ane could she blame,
    An never a word could the lassie say,
          But, I have a good man at hame.

23 'Ye lied, ye lied, my very bonny may,
          Sae loud as I hear you lie!
    For dinna ye mind that misty night
          I was i the bought wi thee?

24 'I ken you by your middle sae jimp,
          An your merry-twinkling ee,
    That ye're the bonny lass i the Cowdenknow,
          An ye may weel seem for to be.'

25 Than he's leapd off his berry-brown steed,
          An he's set that fair may on:
    'Caw out your kye, gude father, yoursel,
          For she's never caw them out again.

20 ca'ing *driving* · kye *cattle*
21 whae's aught *whose is*
22 good man *husband*
25 gude father *father-in-law*

26 'I am the laird of the Oakland hills,
    I hae thirty plows and three,
An I hae gotten the bonniest lass
    That's in a' the south country.'

26 plows *ploughlands*

43

The Shepherd's Dochter

1 There was a shepherd's dochter
    Kept sheep upon yon hill,
And by cam a gay braw gentleman,
    And wad hae had his will.

2 He took her by the milk-white hand,
    And laid her on the ground,
And whan he got his will o her
    He lift her up again.

3 'O syne ye've got your will o me,
    Your will o me ye've taen,
'T is all I ask o you, kind sir,
    Is to tell to me your name.'

4 'Sometimes they call me Jack,' he said,
    'Sometimes they call me John,
But whan I am in the king's court,
    My name is Wilfu Will.'

5 Then he loup on his milk-white steed,
    And straught away he rade,
And she did kilt her petticoats,
    And after him she gaed.

3 syne *since* · 5 loup *mounted* · kilt *tuck up*

6 He never was sae kind as say,
     O lassie, will ye ride?
  Nor ever had she the courage to say,
     O laddie, will ye bide!

7 Until they cam to a wan water,
     Which was called Clyde,
  And then he turned about his horse,
     Said, Lassie, will ye ride?

8 'I learned it in my father's hall,
     I learned it for my weel,
  That whan I come to deep water,
     I can swim as it were an eel.

9 'I learned it in my mother's bower,
     I learned it for my better,
  That whan I come to broad water,
     I can swim like ony otter.'

10 He plunged his steed into the ford,
     And straught way thro he rade,
  And she set in her lilly feet,
     And thro the water wade.

11 And whan she cam to the king's court,
     She tirled on the pin,
  And wha sae ready's the king himsel
     To let the fair maid in?

12 'What is your will wi me, fair maid?
     What is your will wi me?'
  'There is a man into your court
     This day has robbed me.'

6 bide *wait*
10 lilly *lovely*

13 'O has he taen your gold,' he said,
    'Or has he taen your fee?
Or has he stown your maidenhead,
    The flower of your bodye?'

14 'He has na taen my gold, kind sir,
    Nor as little has he taen my fee,
But he has taen my maidenhead,
    The flower of my bodye.'

15 'O gif he be a married man,
    High hangit shall he be,
But gif he be a bachelor,
    His body I'll grant thee.'

16 'Sometimes they call him Jack,' she said,
    'Sometimes they call him John,
But whan he's in the king's court,
    His name is Sweet William.'

17 'There's not a William in a' my court,
    Never a one but three,
And one of them is the Queen's brother;
    I wad laugh gif it war he.'

18 The king called on his merry men,
    By thirty and by three;
Sweet Willie, wha used to be foremost man,
    Was the hindmost a' but three.

19 O he cam cripple, and he cam blind,
    Cam twa-fald oer a tree:
'O be he cripple, or be he blind,
    This very same man is he.'

15 gif *if*
19 twa-fald oer a tree *doubled over a staff*

20 'O whether will ye marry the bonny may,
      Or hang on the gallows-tree?'
   'O I will rather marry the bonny may,
      Afore that I do die.'

21 But he took out a purse of gold,
      Weel locked in a glove:
   'O tak ye that, my bonny may,
      And seek anither love.'

22 'O I will hae none o your gold,' she says,
      'Nor as little ony of your fee,
   But I will hae your ain body,
      The king has granted me.'

23 O he took out a purse of gold,
      A purse of gold and store;
   'O tak ye that, fair may,' he said,
      'Frae me ye'll neer get mair.'

24 'O haud your tongue, young man,' she says,
      'And I pray you let me be;
   For I will hae your ain body,
      The king has granted me.'

25 He mounted her on a bonny bay horse,
      Himsel on the silver grey;
   He drew his bonnet out oer his een,
      He whipt and rade away.

26 O whan they cam to yon nettle bush,
      The nettles they war spread:
   'O an my mither war but here,' she says,
      'These nettles she wad sned.'

21 locked *fastened*
23 store *treasure* · may *maid*
25 out oer *over*
26 an *if* · sned *cut (for food)*

27 'O an I had drank the wan water
　　Whan I did drink the wine,
That eer a shepherd's dochter
　　Should hae been a love o mine!'

28 'O may be I'm a shepherd's dochter,
　　And may be I am nane;
But you might hae ridden on your ways,
　　And hae let me alane.'

29 O whan they cam unto yon mill,
　　She heard the mill clap:

. . . .
. . . .

30 'Clap on, clap on, thou bonny mill,
　　Weel may thou, I say,
For mony a time thou's filled my pock
　　Wi baith oat-meal and grey.'

31 'O an I had drank the wan water
　　Whan I did drink the wine,
That eer a shepherd's dochter
　　Should hae been a love o mine!'

32 'O may be I'm a shepherd's dochter,
　　And may be I am nane;
But you might hae ridden on your ways,
　　And hae let me alane.

33 'But yet I think a fitter match
　　Could scarcely gang thegither
Than the King of France's auld dochter
　　And the Queen of Scotland's brither.'

29 clap *clack*
30 pock *bag* · oat-meal and grey *oat-meal
(white meal) and barley-meal (grey meal)*
33 auld *eldest*

44

The Shepherd's Son

1 There was a shepherd's son
    Kept sheep upon a hill;
He laid his pipe and crook aside,
    And there he slept his fill.
        Sing, Fal deral, etc.

2 He looked east, he looked west,
    Then gave an under-look,
And there he spyed a lady fair,
    Swimming in a brook.

3 He raisd his head frae his green bed,
    And then approachd the maid;
'Put on your claiths, my dear,' he says,
    'And be ye not afraid.

4 ''T is fitter for a lady fair
    To sew her silken seam
Than to get up in a May morning
    And strive against the stream.'

5 'If you'll not touch my mantle,
    And let my claiths alane,
Then I'll give you as much money
    As you can carry hame.'

6 'O I'll not touch your mantle,
    And I'll let your claiths alane;
But I'll tak you out of the clear water,
    My dear, to be my ain.'

2 under-look *covert look*

7 And when she out of the water came,
    He took her in his arms:
'Put on your claiths, my dear,' he says,
    'And hide those lovely charms.'

8 He mounted her on a milk-white steed,
    Himself upon anither,
And all along the way they rode,
    Like sister and like brither.

9 When she came to her father's yate
    She tirled at the pin,
And ready stood the porter there,
    To let this fair maid in.

10 And when the gate was opened,
    So nimbly's she whipt in;
'Pough! you're a fool without,' she says,
    'And I'm a maid within.

11 'Then fare ye well, my modest boy,
    I thank you for your care;
But had you done what you should do,
    I neer had left you there.'

12 'Oh I'll cast aff my hose and shoon,
    And let my feet gae bare,
And gin I meet a bonny lass,
    Hang me if her I spare.'

13 'In that do as you please,' she says,
    'But you shall never more
Have the same opportunity;'
    With that she shut the door.

14 There is a gude auld proverb,
        I've often heard it told,
    He that would not when he might,
        He should not when he would.

45

The Earl of Errol

1 O Errol's place is a bonny place,
        It stands upon yon plain;
    The flowers on it grow red and white,
        The apples red and green.
            The ranting o't and the danting o't,
                According as ye ken,
            The thing they ca the danting o't,
                Lady Errol lies her lane.

2 O Errol's place is a bonny place,
        It stands upon yon plain;
    But what's the use of Errol's place?
        He's no like other men.

3 'As I cam in by yon canal,
        And by yon bowling-green,
    I might hae pleased the best Carnegy
        That ever bore that name.

4 'As sure's your name is Kate Carnegy,
        And mine is Gibbie Hay,
    I'll gar your father sell his land,
        Your tocher for to pay.'

1 ranting *merry-making* · danting *caressing*
4 tocher *dowry*

5 'To gar my father sell his land,
        Would it not be a sin,
    To give it to a naughtless lord
        That couldna get a son?'

6 Now she is on to Edinburgh,
        For to try the law,
    And Errol he has followed her,
        His manhood for to shaw.

7 Then out it spake her sister,
        Whose name was Lady Jane;
    'Had I been Lady Errol,' she says,
        'Or come of sic a clan,
    I would not in this public way
        Have sham'd my own gudeman.'

8 But Errol got it in his will
        To choice a maid himsel,
    And he has taen a country-girl,
        Came in her milk to sell.

9 He took her by the milk-white hand,
        And led her up the green,
    And twenty times he kissd her there,
        Before his lady's een.

10 He took her by the milk-white hand,
        And led her up the stair;
    Says, Thrice three hundred pounds I'll gie
        To you to bear an heir.

11 He kept her there into a room
        Three quarters of a year,
    And when the three quarters were out
        A braw young son she bear.

5 sin *shame* · naughtless *worthless* · get *beget*
7 gudeman *husband* · 8 choice *choose*

12 'Tak hame your daughter, Carnegy,
  And put her till a man,
 For Errol he cannot please her,
  Nor any of his men.'

46

Lord Jamie Douglas

1 O waly, waly up the bank!
  And waly, waly down the brae!
 And waly by yon river side,
  Where me and my lord was wont to gae!

2 An I had wit what I wit now,
  Before I came over the river Tay,
 I would hae staid at Lord Torchard's yetts,
  And I micht hae been his own lady gay.

3 When I lay sick, and was very sick,
  A friend of mine came me to see;
 When our Blacklywood told it in my lord's ears
  That he staid too long in chamber with me.

4 Woe be to thee, thou Blacklywood!
  I wish an ill death may thou die;
 For thou's been the first and occasion last
  That put strife between my good lord and me.

5 When my father he heard of this,
  His heart was like for to break in three;
 He sent fourscore of his soldiers brave
  For to take me home to mine own countree.

1 waly *lament* · 2 wit *known, know*

6　In the morning when I arose,
　　　My bonnie palace for to see,
　I came unto my lord's room-door,
　　　But he would not speak one word to me.

7　'Come down the stair, my lord Jamie Douglas,
　　　Come down and speak one word with me;
　I'll set thee in a chair of gold,
　　　And the never a penny it will cost thee.'

8　'When cockle-shells grow silver bells,
　　　And grass grows over the highest tree,
　When frost and snaw turns fiery bombs,
　　　Then will I come down and drink wine with thee.'

9　O what need I care for Jamie Douglas
　　　More than he needs to care for me?
　For the Lord of Murray's my father dear,
　　　And the Duke of York's daughter my mother be.

10　Thou thocht that I was just like thyself,
　　　And took every one that I did see;
　But I can swear by the heavens above
　　　That I never knew a man but thee.

11　But fare thee weel, my lord Jamie Douglas!
　　　And fare you weel, my sma childer three!
　God grant your father grace to be kind
　　　Till I see you all in my own countrie.

12　Quickly, quickly then rose he up,
　　　And quickly, quickly cam he down;
　When I was in my coaches set,
　　　He made his trumpets all to sound.

11 childer *children*

13　As we came in by Edinburgh town,
　　　　My loving father came to meet me,
　　With trumpets sounding on every side;
　　　　But it was not comfort at all to me.

14　'O hold your tongue, my daughter dear,
　　　　And of your weeping pray let abee;
　　A bill of divorcement I'll to him send,
　　　　And a better lord I will chose for thee.'

15　'Hold your tongue, my father dear,
　　　　And of your flattery pray let abee;
　　I'll never lye in another man's arms,
　　　　Since my Jamie Douglas has forsaken me.'

16　It's often said in a foreign land
　　　　That the hawk she flies far from her nest;
　　It's often said, and it's very true,
　　　　He's far from me this day that I luve best.

14 let abee *cease*

47

The Laird o' Drum

1　The Laird o' Drum's a hunting gone
　　　　All in a morning early
　　And he espied a weel-faured maid
　　　　She was shearin' her father's barley.

2　Thou bonnie maid thou weel-faurd maid
　　　　Oh will ye fancy me, O
　　Oh will ye fancy the Laird o' Drum
　　　　And let your shearin' be O.

1 weel-faured *good-looking* · shearin' *cutting,
harvesting*

3 I wouldna fancy the Laird o' Drum
    He is far above by degree O
For I'm not fitted his bride to be
    And his miss I wad scorn to be O.

4 You'll cast aff the goon o' gray
    Put on the silk and scarlet
And you will be the Lady o' Drum
    And neither miss nor harlot.

5 Your silken goons I canna wear
    They wad rustle at my heels O
But I will wear the colour o' my ewe,
    For it suits my body weel O.

6 Your china cups I canna wash
    Nor mak' a cup o' tea O
But I can milk the cow or the ewe
    Wi the cogie on my knee O.

7 My father is an auld shepherd
    Keeps sheep on yonder hill O
And ilka thing that he bids me do
    I work aye at his will O.

8 He's taen her to the auld shepherd
    Keeps sheep on yonder hill O
Says, Oh but you have a bonny daughter
    And oh, but I like her weel O.

9 She'll winnow yer corn, she'll sift yer meal
    And drive to mill or kiln O
And in time o' need, she'll saddle yer steed
    And she'll draw yer boots hersel O.

3 miss *mistress* · 6 cogie *wooden container*
7 ilka *every* · 9 draw *pull off*

10   But who will bake my bridal bread
          And who will brew my ale O
      And who will welcome my love in
          It's more than I can tell O.

11   The baker will bake your bridal bread
          The brewer will brew your ale O
      And fa' will welcome your love in,
          You can welcome her in yersel' O.

12   There was four and twenty lairds and lords
          Stood at the gates o' Drum O
      But nane o' them a' put his hand to his hat
          To welcome the shepherd's daughter in O.

13   But he's taen her by the milk white hand
          And he's led her gently in O
      And he's given her the keys into her hand
          And he's styled her Lady o' Drum O.

14   Out and spoke his brother John
          An angry man was he O
      You've married a wife my brother dear,
          She'll be an affront to all your kin O.

15   The first wife that I married
          She was far above my degree O
      I couldna enter the room where she was
          Without my hat down by my knee O.

16   Now I've married a wife to win my bread
          But you've married one to spend O
      And as long as my head shall carry my hat
          She'll aye be Lady o' Drum O.

16 win *earn*

17 When a' was eaten and a' was drunken
    And all were bound for bed O
  The Laird o' Drum and the shepherd's daughter
    They were baith in ae bed laid O.

18 If ye had been as good as me
    As good as the Laird o' Drum O
  We would have walked the streets last night
    Among good company O.

19 I told ye afore ye mairriet me
    Ye were far above my degree O
  But noo that we're mairriet and in ae bed laid
    Ye'll be forced to be deein wi me O.

20 When Adam and Eve our first parents
    Did eat the forbidden tree O
  O where were a' your gentry then
    Am not I just as good as thee O.

21 Gin ye were deid and I were deid
    And baith in ae grave laid O
  And seven lang years had passed and gane
    They wad scarce ken your dust by mine O.

21 scarce ken your dust by mine *scarcely be able to
distinguish your dust from mine*

48

The Cooper of Fife

1 There was a wee cooper who lived in Fife,
   Nickity, nackity, noo, noo, noo
And he has gotten a gentle wife.
   Hey Willie Wallacky, how John Dougall,
   Alane, quo Rushety, roue, roue, roue

2 She wadna bake, nor she wadna brew,
   For the spoiling o her comely hue.

3 She wadna card, nor she wadna spin,
   For the shaming o her gentle kin.

4 She wadna wash, nor she wadna wring,
   For the spoiling o her gouden ring.

5 The cooper's awa to his woo-pack
   And has laid a sheep-skin on his wife's back.

6 'It's I'll no thrash ye, for your proud kin,
   But I will thrash my ain sheep-skin.'

7 'Oh, I will bake, and I will brew,
   And never mair think on my comely hue.

8 'Oh, I will card, and I will spin,
   And never mair think on my gentle kin.

9 'Oh, I will wash, and I will wring,
   And never mair think on my gouden ring.'

10 A' ye wha hae gotten a gentle wife
   Send ye for the wee cooper o Fife.

1 gentle *belonging to the gentry*
5 woo-pack *wool-pack.*

49

Get Up and Bar the Door

1 It fell about the Martinmas time,
    And a gay time it was then,
When our goodwife got puddings to make,
    And she's boild them in the pan.

2 The wind sae cauld blew south and north,
    And blew into the floor;
Quoth our goodman to our goodwife,
    'Gae out and bar the door.'

3 'My hand is in my hussyfskap,
    Goodman, as ye may see;
An it shoud nae be barrd this hundred year,
    It's no be barrd for me.'

4 They made a paction tween them twa,
    They made it firm and sure,
That the first word whaeer shoud speak,
    Shoud rise and bar the door.

5 Then by there came two gentlemen,
    At twelve o clock at night,
And they could neither see house nor hall,
    Nor coal nor candle-light.

6 'Now whether is this a rich man's house,
    Or whether is it a poor?'
But neer a word wad ane o them speak,
    For barring of the door.

1 goodwife *mistress of the house*
2 goodman *master of the house*
3 hussyfskap *housewifery*
4 paction *pact*
5 coal *fire*

7　And first they ate the white puddings,
　　　　And then they ate the black;
　　Tho muckle thought the goodwife to hersel,
　　　　Yet neer a word she spake.

8　Then said the one unto the other,
　　　　'Here, man, tak ye my knife;
　　Do ye tak aff the auld man's beard,
　　　　And I'll kiss the goodwife.'

9　'But there's nae water in the house,
　　　　And what shall we do than?'
　　'What ails ye at the pudding-broo,
　　　　That boils into the pan?'

10　O up then started our goodman,
　　　　An angry man was he:
　　'Will ye kiss my wife before my een,
　　　　And scad me wi pudding-bree?'

11　Then up and started our goodwife,
　　　　Gied three skips on the floor:
　　'Goodman, you've spoken the foremost word,
　　　　Get up and bar the door.'

9 what ails ye at the pudding-broo *what's your
objection to the pudding water*
10 scad *scald*

50

Our Goodman

1 Hame came our goodman,
    And hame came he,
And then he saw a saddle-horse,
    Where nae horse should be.

2 'What's this now, goodwife?
    What's this I see?
How came this horse here,
    Without the leave o me?'

Recitative. 'A horse?' quo she.
    'Ay, a horse,' quo he.

3 'Shame fa your cuckold face,
    Ill mat ye see!
'T is naething but a broad sow,
    My minnie sent to me.'

'A broad sow?' quo he.
'Ay, a sow,' quo shee.

4 'Far hae I ridden,
    And farer hae I gane,
But a sadle on a sow's back
    I never saw nane.

5 Hame came our goodman,
    And hame came he;
He spy'd a pair of jack-boots,
    Where nae boots should be.

1 goodman *master of the house*
2 goodwife *mistress of the house ·*
quo *said*
3 mat *may ·* broad sow *sow with a*
litter · minnie *mother*
4 nane *at all, ever*

6 'What's this now, goodwife?
    What's this I see?
How came these boots here,
    Without the leave o me?'

'Boots?' quo she.
'Ay, boots,' quo he.

7 'Shame fa your cuckold face,
    And ill mat ye see!
It's but a pair of water-stoups,
    My minnie sent to me.'

'Water-stoups?' quo he.
'Ay, water-stoups,' quo she.

8 'Far hae I ridden,
    And farer hae I gane,
But siller spurs on water-stoups
    I saw never nane.'

9 Hame came our goodman,
    And hame came he,
And he saw a sword,
    Whare a sword should na be.

10 'What's this now, goodwife?
    What's this I see?
How came this sword here,
    Without the leave o me?'

'A sword?' quo she.
'Ay, a sword,' quo he.

7 water-stoups *buckets or pitchers for water*
8 siller *silver*

11 'Shame fa your cuckold face,
    Ill mat ye see!
It's but a porridge-spurtle,
    My minnie sent to me.'

'A spurtle?' quo he.
'Ay, a spurtle,' quo she.

12 'Far hae I ridden,
    And farer hae I gane,
But siller-handed spurtles
    I saw never nane.'

13 Hame came our goodman,
    And hame came he;
There he spy'd a powderd wig,
    Whare nae wig shoud be.

14 'What's this now, goodwife?
    What's this I see?
How came this wig here,
    Without the leave o me?'

'A wig?' quo she.
'Ay, a wig,' quo he.

15 'Shame fa your cuckold face,
    And ill mat you see!
'T is naething but a clocken-hen,
    My minnie sent to me.'

'Clocken hen?' quo he.
'Ay, clocken hen,' quo she.

11 porridge-spurtle *stick for stirring porridge*
12 siller-handed *silver-handled*
15 clocken-hen *sitting hen*

16 'Far hae I ridden,
       And farer hae I gane,
   But powder on a clocken-hen
       I saw never nane.'

17 Hame came our goodman,
       And hame came he,
   And there he saw a muckle coat,
       Whare nae coat shoud be.

18 'What's this now, goodwife?
       What's this I see?
   How came this coat here,
       Without the leave o me?'

   'A coat?' quo she.
   'Ay, a coat,' quo he.

19 'Shame fa your cuckold face,
       Ill mat ye see!
   It's but a pair o blankets,
       My minnie sent to me.'

   'Blankets?' quo he.
   'Ay, blankets,' quo she.

20 'Far hae I ridden,
       And farer hae I gane,
   But buttons upon blankets
       I saw never nane.'

21 Ben went our goodman,
       And ben went he,
   And there he spy'd a sturdy man,
       Whare nae man shoud be.

   21 ben *to the inner room*

22 'What's this now, goodwife?
  What's this I see?
How came this man here,
  Without the leave o me?'

 'A man?' quo she.
 'Ay, a man,' quo he.

23 'Poor blind body,
  And blinder mat ye be!
It's a new milking-maid,
  My mither sent to me.'

 'A maid?' quo he.
 'Ay, a maid,' quo she.

24 'Far hae I ridden,
  And farer hae I gane,
But lang-bearded maidens
  I saw never nane.'

51

The Farmer's Curst Wife

1 The auld Deil cam to the man at the pleugh,
  Rumchy ae de aidie
Saying, I wish ye gude luck at the making o yer sheugh.
  Mushy toorin an ant tan aira.

2 'It's neither your oxen nor you that I crave;
It's that old scolding woman, it's her I must have.'

3 'Ye're welcome to her wi a' my gude heart;
I wish you and her it's never may part.'

1 Deil *Devil* · sheugh *furrow*

[177]

4 She jumped on to the auld Deil's back,
   And he carried her awa like a pedlar's pack.

5 He carried her on till he cam to hell's door,
   He gaed her a kick till she landed in the floor.

6 She saw seven wee deils a sitting in a raw,
   She took up a mell and she murdered them a'.

7 A wee reekit deil lookit owre the wa:
   'O tak her awa, or she'll ruin us a'.'

8 'O what to do wi her I canna weel tell;
   She's no fit for heaven, and she'll no bide in hell.'

* * * * *

9 She jumpit on to the auld Deil's back,
   And he carried her back like a pedlar's pack.

* * * * *

10 She was seven years gaun, and seven years comin,
   And she cried for the sowens she left in the pot.

6 raw *row* · mell *wooden hammer* · 7 reekit *smoky* · 8 bide *stay*
10 cried for *demanded* · sowens *dish made from oats*

52

Bog o' Gight

1 Will you go to the Highlands my bonnie love
   Will you go to the Highlands wi' Geordie
And you'll tak' the high road and I'll tak the low
   And I'll be in the Highlands afore you.

2 I wad far rather stay on the bonny banks o' Spey
      And see a' the fish boaties rowin
  Before I wad go to your high Highland hills
      And hear a' yer white kye lowin.

3 He had not been in the high highland hills
      Months but barely three
  Before he was cast into prison strong
      For hunting the deer and the roe O.

4 Where will I find a bonny little boy
      Who will run an errand shortly
  And who will run on to the bonny Bog o' Gight
      Wi' a letter to Gighty's lady O.

5 Here am I a bonny little boy
      Who will run an errand shortly
  And will run on to the bonny Bog o' Gight
      Wi' a letter to Gighty's lady.

6 When that you come where the grass grows long
      Slack your shoes and run O
  When that you come where the bridge is broke
      Bend your bow and swim O.

7 When that you come to Gighty's gates
      Stop neither to chap nor call O
  But bend your bow right clean to your breast
      And jump right over the wall O.

8 When that he came where the grass grew long
      He slacked his shoes and ran O
  And when he came where the bridge was broke
      He bent his bow and swam O.

2 kye *cattle* · 6 slack *slacken* · 7 chap *knock*

9 When that he came to Gighty's gates
      He stopped neither to chap nor to call O
  But he's bent his bow right close to his breast
      And jumped right over the wall O.

10 When she looked the letter upon
      A loud loud laugh laughed she O
  But ere she had the half o't read
      The saut tear blinded her e'e O.

11 Go saddle to me the black horse she cried
      The brown never rode so boldly
  Until I ride to Edinburgh toon
      To see and get life for my Geordie.

12 When that she came to yon ford mou
      The boatman he wasna ready
  But she clasped her hands and round her high horse neck
      And she swam the ferry shortly.

13 When that she came to the pier o' Leith
      The poor people they stood many
  She parted the yellow gold them among
      Bade them pray for the life o' her Geordie.

14 When that she cam' to Edinburgh toon
      The nobles they stood many
  And every one had his hat on his heid
      But hat in hand stood her Geordie.

15 Oh, has he killed or has he brunt
      Oh, has he killed any
  Or what has my love Geordie done
      That he's going to be hanged shortly.

12 mou *mouth* · 13 parted *distributed* · 15 brunt *burnt*

16 He hasna killed, nor has he brunt
    Nor has he killed any
But he's been a-hunting the king's own deer
    And he's going to be hanged shortly.

17 Will the yellow gold buy off my bonnie love
    Will the yellow gold buy off my Geordie
It's five hundred crowns if ye wad pay doon
    You'll get the hat on your Geordie.

18 She's taen the red mantle frae her neck
    She's spread it oot fou bonny
And she's taen the hat oot o' Geordie's hand
    And she's begged roand them shortly.

19 Some gave her crowns and some gave her pounds
    And some gave her hundreds many
And the king himsel' gien her one hundred more
    To get the hat on her Geordie.

20 When she was on her high horse set
    And in behind her Geordie
The bird ne'er sang sae sweetly on the bush
    As she did behind her Geordie.

21 Out an spake an Irish duke
    An auld bow-legged body
Says I wish that Gighty had lost his heid
    An I had gotten his lady.

22 She turned her high horse quickly about
    And O but wasna' she saucy
Says 'Pokes be upon your Irish face
    For ye never could compare wi my Geordie.'

22 pokes *pox*

[181]

23 First I wis lady o' bonny Auchindoun
    And next I was Lady o' Gartly
But noo I'm guidwife o' the bonny Bog o' Gight
    And I begged the life o' my Geordie.

23 guidwife *mistress*

53

The Laird o Logie

1 I will sing, if ye will hearken,
    If ye will hearken unto me;
The king has taen a poor prisoner,
    The wanton laird o Young Logie.

2 Young Logie's laid in Edinburgh chapel,
    Carmichael's the keeper o the key;
And May Margaret's lamenting sair,
    A' for the love of Young Logie.

3 'Lament, lament na, May Margaret,
    And of your weeping let me be;
For ye maun to the king himsell,
    To seek the life of Young Logie.'

4 May Margaret has kilted her green cleiding,
    And she has curld back her yellow hair:
'If I canna get Young Logie's life,
    Farewell to Scotland for evermair!'

5 When she came before the king,
    She knelit lowly on her knee:
'O what's the matter, May Margaret?
    And what needs a' this courtesie?'

6 'A boon, a boon, my noble liege,
  A boon, a boon, I beg o thee,
 And the first boon that I come to crave
  Is to grant me the life of Young Logie.'

7 'O na, O na, May Margaret,
  Forsooth, and so it mauna be;
 For a' the gowd o fair Scotland
  Shall not save the life of Young Logie.'

8 But she has stown the king's redding-kaim,
  Likewise the queen her wedding knife,
 And sent the tokens to Carmichael,
  To cause Young Logie get his life.

9 She sent him a purse o the red gowd,
  Another o the white monie;
 She sent him a pistol for each hand,
  And bade him shoot when he gat free.

10 When he came to the Tolbooth stair,
  There he let his volley flee;
 It made the king in his chamber start,
  Een in the bed where he might be.

11 'Gae out, gae out, my merrymen a',
  And bid Carmichael come speak to me;
 For I'll lay my life the pledge o that
  That yon's the shot o Young Logie.'

12 When Carmichael came before the king,
  He fell low down upon his knee;
 The very first word that the king spake
  Was, Where's the laird of Young Logie?

8 redding-kaim *comb* · queen her *queen's*
9 white monie *silver*

13 Carmichael turnd him round about,
       I wot the tear blinded his ee:
    'There came a token frae your Grace
       Has taen away the laird frae me.'

14 'Hast thou playd me that, Carmichael?
       And hast thou playd me that?' quoth he;
    'The morn the Justice Court's to stand,
       And Logie's place ye maun supplie.'

15 Carmichael's awa to Margaret's bower,
       Even as fast as he may dree:
    'O if Young Logie be within,
       Tell him to come and speak with me.'

16 May Margaret turnd her round about,
       I wot a loud laugh laughed she:
    'The egg is chippd, the bird is flown,
       Ye'll see nae mair of Young Logie.'

17 The tane is shipped at the pier of Leith,
       The tother at the Queen's Ferrie,
  And she's gotten a father to her bairn,
       The wanton laird of Young Logie.

15 may *could*

54

Johnie Scott

1 Johnie Scott's a hunting gone,
       To England woods so wild,
  Until the king's old dochter dear
       She goes to him with child.

1 old *eldest*

2 'If she be with bairn,' her mother says,
  'As I trew weel she be,
 We'll put her in a dark dungeon,
  And hunger her till she die.'

3 'If she be with bairn,' her father says,
  'As oh forbid she be!
 We'll put her in a prison strong,
  And try the veritie.'

4 The king did write a long letter,
  Sealed it with his own hand,
 And he sent it to Johnie Scot,
  To speak at his command.

5 When Johnie read this letter long,
  The tear blindit his ee:
 'I must away to Old England;
  King Edward writes for me.'

6 Out and spak his mother dear,
  She spoke aye in time:
 Son, if thou go to Old England,
  I fear thou'll neer come hame.

7 Out and spoke a Scotish prince,
  And a weel spoke man was he:
 Here's four and twenty o my braw troops,
  To bear thee companie.

8 Away they gade, awa they rade,
  Away they rade so slie;
 There was not a maried man that day
  In Johnie's companie.

2 trew *believe* · hunger *starve*
3 try the veritie *get at the truth*
8 slie *cunningly*

9   The first good town that they passed thro,
        They made their bells to ring;
    The next good town that they passed thro,
        They made their music sing.

10 The next gude town that they passed thro,
        They made their drums beat round,
    The king and a' his gay armies
        Admiring at the sound.

11 When they came to the king's court,
        They travelled round about,
    And there he spied his own true-love,
        At a window looking out.

12 'O fain wald I come down,' she says,
        'Of that ye needna dout;
    But my garters they're of cauld, cauld iron,
        And I can no win out.

13 'My garters they're of cauld, cauld iron,
        And it is very cold;
    My breast-plate is of sturdy steel,
        Instead o beaten gold.'

14 Out and spoke the king himsell,
        And an angry man was he:
    The fairest lady in a' my court,
        She goes with child to thee.

15 'If your old doughter be with child,
        As I trew weel she be,
    I'le make it heir of a' my land,
        And her my gay lady.'

16 'There is a Talliant in my court,
       This day he's killed three;
   And gin the morn by ten o'clock
       He'll kill thy men and thee.'

17 Johnie took sword into his hand,
       And walked cross the plain;
   There was many a weeping lady there,
       To see young Johnie slain.

18 The Talliant never knowing this,
       Now he'll be Johnie's dead,
   But, like unto a swallow swift,
       He flew out owre his head.

19 Johnie was a valliant man,
       Weel taught in war was he,
   And on the point of his broad sword
       The Talliant stickit he.

20 Johnie took sword into his hand,
       And walked cross the plain:
   'Are there here any moe of your English dogs
       That's wanting to be slain?

21 'A priest, a priest,' young Johnie cries,
       'To wed my bride and me;'
   'A clerk, a clerk,' her father cries,
       'To tell her tocher wi.'

22 'I'm wanting none of your gold,' he says,
       'As little of your gear;
   But give me just mine own true-love,
       I think I've won her dear.'

16 Talliant *Italian*
18 dead *death* · out owre *right over*
19 stickit *stuck*
20 moe *more*
21 tell *reckon* · tocher *dowry*.

23 Johnie sets horn into his mouth,
  And he blew loud and schrill;
 The honour it's to Scotland come,
  Sore against England's will.

55

Lang Johnny Moir

1 There lives a man in Rynie's land,
  Anither in Auchindore,
 The bravest lad amo them a'
  Was lang Johnny Moir.

2 Young Johnny was an airy blade,
  Fu sturdy, stout, and strang;
 The sword that hang by Johnny's side
  Was just full ten feet lang.

3 Young Johnny was a clever youth,
  Fu sturdy, stout, and wight,
 Just full three yards around the waist,
  And fourteen feet in hight.

4 But if a' be true they tell me now,
  And a' be true I hear,
 Young Johnny's on to Lundan gane,
  The king's banner to bear.

5 He hadna been in fair Lundan
  But twalmonths twa or three
 Till the fairest lady in a' Lundan
  Fell in love wi young Johnny.

1 bravest *finest* · 3 clever *vigorous* · wight *active*

6   This news did sound thro Lundan town,
        Till it came to the king
    That the muckle Scot had fa'in in love
        Wi his daughter, Lady Jean.

7   Whan the king got word o that,
        A solemn oath sware he,
    This weighty Scot sall strait a rope,
        And hanged he shall be.

8   When Johnny heard the sentence past,
        A light laugh then gae he:
    'While I hae strength to wield my blade,
        Ye darena a' hang me.'

9   The English dogs were cunning rogues;
        About him they did creep,
    And gae him draps o lodomy
        That laid him fast asleep.

10 Whan Johnny wakend frae his sleep
        A sorry heart had he;
    His jaws and hands in iron bands,
        His feet in fetters three.

11 'O whar will I get a little wee boy
        Will work for meat and fee,
    That will rin on to my uncle,
        At the foot of Benachie?'

12 'Here am I, a little wee boy
        Will work for meat and fee,
    That will rin on to your uncle,
        At the foot of Benachie.'

7 strait *stretch*
9 lodomy *laudanum*
11 meat *food* · fee *hire*

[189]

13　'Whan ye come whar grass grows green,
　　　　Slack your shoes and rin;
　　And whan ye come whar water's strong,
　　　　Ye'll bend your bow and swim.

14　'And whan ye come to Benachie
　　　　Ye'll neither chap nor ca;
　　Sae well's ye'll ken auld Johnny there,
　　　　Three feet abeen them a'.

15　'Ye'll gie to him this braid letter,
　　　　Seald wi my faith and troth,
　　And ye'll bid him bring alang wi him
　　　　The body Jock o Noth.'

16　Whan he came whar grass grew green,
　　　　He slackt his shoes and ran;
　　And whan he came whar water's strong
　　　　He bent his bow and swam.

17　And whan he came to Benachie
　　　　Did neither chap nor ca;
　　Sae well's he kent auld Johnny there,
　　　　Three feet abeen them a'.

18　'What news, what news, my little wee boy?
　　　　Ye never were here before;'
　　'Nae news, nae news, but a letter from
　　　　Your nephew, Johnny Moir.

19　'Ye'll take here this braid letter,
　　　　Seald wi his faith and troth,
　　And ye're bidden bring alang wi you
　　　　The body Jock o Noth.'

13 slack *slacken* · 14 chap *knock*
15 body *person*

20 Benachie lyes very low,
         The tap o Noth lyes high;
     For a' the distance that's between,
         He heard auld Johnny cry.

21 Whan on the plain these champions met,
         Twa grizly ghosts to see,
     There were three feet between their brows,
         And shoulders were yards three.

22 These men they ran ower hills and dales,
         And ower mountains high,
     Till they came on to Lundan town,
         At the dawn o the third day.

23 And whan they came to Lundan town
         The yetts were lockit wi bands,
     And wha were there but a trumpeter,
         Wi trumpet in his hands?

24 'What is the matter, ye keepers all?
         Or what's the matter within
     That the drums do beat and bells do ring,
         And make sic dolefu din?'

25 'There's naething the matter,' the keeper said,
         'There's naething the matter to thee,
     But a weighty Scot to strait the rope,
         And the morn he maun die.'

26 'O open the yetts, ye proud keepers,
         Ye'll open without delay;'
     The trembling keeper, smiling, said,
         'O I hae not the key.'

21 grizly ghosts *terrible apparitions*
23 bands *chains*
24 dolefu *sad*
25 the morn *tomorrow*

27 'Ye'll open the yetts, ye proud keepers,
    Ye'll open without delay,
Or here is a body at my back
    Frae Scotland has brought the key.'

28 'Ye'll open the yetts,' says Jock o Noth,
    'Ye'll open them at my call;'
Then wi his foot he has drove in
    Three yards braid o the wall.

29 As they gaed in by Drury Lane,
    And down by the town's hall,
And there they saw young Johnny Moir
    Stand on their English wall.

30 'Ye're welcome here, my uncle dear,
    Ye're welcome unto me;
Ye'll loose the knot, and slack the rope,
    And set me frae the tree.'

31 'Is it for murder, or for theft?
    Or is it for robberie?
If it is for ony heinous crime,
    There's nae remeid for thee.'

32 'It's nae for murder, nor for theft,
    Nor yet for robberie;
A' is for the loving a gay lady
    They're gaun to gar me die.'

33 'O whar's thy sword,' says Jock o Noth,
    'Ye brought frae Scotland wi thee?
I never saw a Scotsman yet
    But coud wield a sword or tree.'

30 set me frae the tree *free me from the gallows*
31 remeid *remedy*
33 tree *spear*

34 'A pox upo their lodomy,
    On me had sic a sway
Four o their men, the bravest four,
    They bore my blade away.'

35 'Bring back his blade,' says Jock o Noth,
    'And freely to him it gie,
Or I hae sworn a black Scot's oath
    I'll gar five million die.

36 'Now whar's the lady?' says Jock o Noth,
    'Sae fain I woud her see;'
'She's lockd up in her ain chamber,
    The king he keeps the key.'

37 So they hae gane before the king,
    With courage bauld and free;
Their armour bright cast sic a light
    That almost dim'd his ee.

38 'O whar's the lady?' says Jock o Noth,
    'Sae fain as I woud her see;
For we are come to her wedding,
    Frae the foot o Benachie.'

39 'O take the lady,' said the king,
    'Ye welcome are for me;
I never thought to see sic men,
    Frae the foot o Benachie.'

40 'If I had kend,' said Jock o Noth,
    'Ye'd wonderd sae muckle at me,
I woud hae brought ane larger far
    By sizes three times three.

34 pox *curse* · on me had sic a sway *had such
power over me*
37 free *spirited*
38 sae fain as I woud her see *I would very
much like to see her*

41 'Likewise if I had thought I'd been
      Sic a great fright to thee,
  I'd brought Sir John o Erskine Park;
      He's thretty feet and three.'

42 'Wae to the little boy,' said the king,
      'Brought tidings unto thee!
  Let all England say what they will,
      High hangèd shall he be.'

43 'O if ye hang the little wee boy
      Brought tidings unto me,
  We shall attend his burial,
      And rewarded ye shall be.'

44 'O take the lady,' said the king,
      'And the boy shall be free;'
  'A priest, a priest,' then Johnny cried,
      'To join my love and me.'

45 'A clerk, a clerk,' the king replied,
      'To seal her tocher wi thee;'
  Out it speaks auld Johnny then,
      These words pronounced he:

46 'I want nae lands and rents at hame,
      I'll ask nae gowd frae thee;
  I am possessd o riches great,
      Hae fifty ploughs and three;
  Likewise fa's heir to ane estate
      At the foot o Benachie.

47 'Hae ye ony masons in this place,
      Or ony at your call,
  That ye may now send some o them
      To build your broken wall?'

45 seal her tocher *draw up a dowry
document and confirm it*
46 ploughs *ploughlands*

48 'Yes, there are masons in this place,
     And plenty at my call;
   But ye may gang frae whence ye came,
     Never mind my broken wall.'

49 They've taen the lady by the hand
     And set her prison-free;
   Wi drums beating, and fifes playing,
     They spent the night wi glee.

50 Now auld Johnny Moir, and young Johnny Moir,
     And Jock o Noth, a' three,
   The English lady, and little wee boy,
     Went a' to Benachie.

49 prison-free *free from prison*

56

The Keach i the Creel

1 A fair young may went up the street,
    Some white-fish for to buy,
  And a bonnie clerk's faen in love wi her,
    And he's followed her by and by, by,
    And he's followed her by and by.

2 'O where live ye, my bonnie lass,
    I pray thee tell to me;
  For gin the nicht were ever sae mirk
    I wad come and visit thee.'

TITLE keach *shaking up*
1 white-fish *light-coloured fish such as cod or haddock*

3 'O my father he aye locks the door,
    My mither keeps the key;
And gin ye were ever sic a wily wight
    Ye canna win in to me.'

4 But the clerk he had ae true brother,
    And a wily wight was he;
And he has made a lang ladder,
    Was thirty steps and three.

5 He has made a cleek but and a creel,
    A creel but and a pin;
And he's away to the chimley-top,
    And he's letten the bonnie clerk in.

6 The auld wife, being not asleep,
    Heard something that was said;
'I'll lay my life,' quo the silly auld wife,
    'There's a man i our dochter's bed.'

7 The auld man he gat owre the bed,
    To see if the thing was true;
But she's ta'en the bonny clerk in her arms,
    And coverd him owre wi blue.

8 'O where are ye gaun now, father?' she says,
    'And where are ye gaun sae late?
Ye've disturbd me in my evening prayers,
    And O but they were sweet!'

9 'O ill betide ye, silly auld wife,
    And an ill death may ye die!
She has the muckle buik in her arms,
    And she's prayin for you and me.'

3 wight *person*
5 cleek but and a creel *hook and also a basket* ·
pin *peg* · chimley-top *chimney-top*
6 silly *foolish* · wife *woman*
9 muckle buik *bible*

10   The auld wife being not asleep,
       Then something mair was said;
    'I'll lay my life,' quo the silly auld wife,
       'There's a man i our dochter's bed.'

11   The auld wife she got owre the bed,
       To see if the thing was true;
    But what the wrack took the auld wife's fit?
       For into the creel she flew.

12   The man that was at the chimley-top,
       Finding the creel was fu,
    He wrappit the rape round his left shouther,
       And fast to him he drew.

13   'O help! O help! O hinny, now, help!
       O help, O hinny, now!
    For him that ye aye wished me to
       He's carryin me off just now.'

14   'O if the foul thief's gotten ye,
       I wish he may keep his haud;
    For a' the lee lang winter nicht
       Ye'll never lie in your bed.'

15   He's towed her up, he's towed her down,
       He's towed her through an through;
    'O Gude assist!' quo the silly auld wife,
       'For I'm just departin now.'

16   He's towed her up, he's towed her down,
       He's gien her a richt down-fa,
    Till every rib i the auld wife's side
       Playd nick-nack on the wa.

11 wrack *devil* · 13 hinny *honey*
14 foul thief's *devil's* · lee lang *livelong*
15 he's towed her up, he's towed her down *he's pulled her up and down* · departin *dying*
16 playd nick-nack on the wa *knocked against the wall with a crack*

17 O the blue, the bonnie, bonnie blue,
    And I wish the blue may do weel!
  And every auld wife that's sae jealous o her dochter,
    May she get a good keach i the creel!

57

The Gay Goss Hawk

1 'O well's me o my gay goss-hawk,
    That he can speak and flee;
  He'll carry a letter to my love,
    Bring back another to me.'

2 'O how can I your true-love ken,
    Or how can I her know?
  Whan frae her mouth I never heard couth,
    Nor wi my eyes her saw.'

3 'O well sal ye my true-love ken,
    As soon as you her see;
  For, of a' the flowrs in fair Englan,
    The fairest flowr is she.

4 'At even at my love's bowr-door
    There grows a bowing birk,
  An sit ye down and sing thereon,
    As she gangs to the kirk.

5 'An four-and-twenty ladies fair
    Will wash and go to kirk,
  But well shall ye my true-love ken,
    For she wears goud on her skirt.

1 well's me o *it's fortunate for me concerning*
2 couth *speech* · 4 birk *birch*

6 'An four-and-twenty gay ladies
    Will to the mass repair,
  But well sal ye my true-love ken,
    For she wears goud in her hair.'

7 O even at that lady's bowr-door
    There grows a bowin birk,
  An she set down and sang thereon,
    As she ged to the kirk.

8 'O eet and drink, my marys a',
    The wine flows you among,
  Till I gang to my shot-window,
    An hear yon bonny bird's song.

9 'Sing on, sing on, my bonny bird,
    The song ye sang the streen,
  For I ken by your sweet singin
    You're frae my true-love sen.'

10 O first he sang a merry song,
    An then he sang a grave,
  An then he peckd his feathers gray,
    To her the letter gave.

11 'Ha, there's a letter frae your love,
    He says he sent you three;
  He canna wait your love langer,
    But for your sake he'll die.

12 'He bids you write a letter to him;
    He says he's sent you five;
  He canno wait your love langer,
    Tho you're the fairest woman alive.'

8 marys *maids* · shot-window *box-window
or hinged window*
9 the streen *yesterday*

13 'Ye bid him bake his bridal-bread,
        And brew his bridal-ale,
    An I'll meet him in fair Scotlan
        Lang, lang or it be stale.'

14 She's doen her to her father dear,
        Fa'n low down on her knee:
    'A boon, a boon, my father dear,
        I pray you, grant it me.'

15 'Ask on, ask on, my daughter,
        An granted it sal be;
    Except ae squire in fair Scotlan,
        An him you sall never see.'

16 'The only boon, my father dear,
        That I do crave of the,
    Is, gin I die in southin lands,
        In Scotland to bury me.

17 'An the firstin kirk that ye come till,
        Ye gar the bells be rung,
    An the nextin kirk that ye come till,
        Ye gar the mess be sung.

18 'An the thirdin kirk that ye come till,
        You deal gold for my sake,
    An the fourthin kirk that ye come till,
        You tarry there till night.'

19 She is doen her to her bigly bowr,
        As fast as she coud fare,
    An she has tane a sleepy draught,
        That she had mixed wi care.

14 doen her *gone*
18 deal *distribute*
19 bigly *fine*

20 She's laid her down upon her bed,
      An soon she's fa'n asleep,
   And soon oer every tender limb
      Cauld death began to creep.

21 Whan night was flown, an day was come,
      Nae ane that did her see
   But thought she was as surely dead
      As ony lady coud be.

22 Her father an her brothers dear
      Gard make to her a bier;
   The tae half was guide red gold,
      The tither o silver clear.

23 Her mither an her sisters fair
      Gard work for her a sark;
   The tae half was o cambrick fine,
      The tither o needle wark.

24 The firstin kirk that they came till,
      They gard the bells be rung,
   An the nextin kirk that they came till,
      They gard the mess be sung.

25 The thirdin kirk that they came till,
      They dealt gold for her sake,
   An the fourthin kirk that they came till,
      Lo, there they met her make!

26 'Lay down, lay down the bigly bier,
      Lat me the dead look on;'
   Wi cherry cheeks and ruby lips
      She lay an smil'd on him.

23 sark *burial garment*
25 make *mate*

27 'O ae sheave o your bread, true-love,
   An ae glass o your wine,
For I hae fasted for your sake
   These fully days is nine.

28 'Gang hame, gang hame, my seven bold brothers,
   Gang hame and sound your horn;
An ye may boast in southin lans
   Your sister's playd you scorn.'

27 sheave *slice*
28 southin *southern* · playd you scorn *made a mock of you*

58

Love Gregor

1 'O wha will shoe my fu fair foot?
   And wha will glove my hand?
And wha will lace my middle jimp,
   Wi the new made London band?

2 'And wha will kaim my yellow hair,
   Wi the new made silver kaim?
And wha will father my young son,
   Till Love Gregor come hame?'

3 'Your father will shoe your fu fair foot,
   Your mother will glove your hand;
Your sister will lace your middle jimp
   Wi the new made London band.

4 'Your brother will kaim your yellow hair,
   Wi the new made silver kaim;
And the king of heaven will father your bairn,
   Till Love Gregor come haim.'

1 middle jimp *slender waist*

5 'But I will get a bonny boat,
    And I will sail the sea,
For I maun gang to Love Gregor,
    Since he canno come hame to me.'

6 O she has gotten a bonny boat,
    And sailld the sa't sea fame;
She langd to see her ain true-love,
    Since he could no come hame.

7 'O row your boat, my mariners,
    And bring me to the land,
For yonder I see my love's castle,
    Closs by the sa't sea strand.'

8 She has taen her young son in her arms,
    And to the door she's gone,
And lang she's knocked and sair she ca'd,
    But answer got she none.

9 'O open the door, Love Gregor,' she says,
    'O open, and let me in;
For the wind blaws thro my yellow hair,
    And the rain draps oer my chin.'

10 'Awa, awa, ye ill woman,
    You'r nae come here for good;
You'r but some witch, or wile warlock,
    Or mer-maid of the flood.'

11 'I am neither a witch nor a wile warlock,
    Nor mer-maid of the sea,
I am Fair Annie of Rough Royal;
    O open the door to me.'

10 wile warlock *vile wizard*

12   'Gin ye be Annie of Rough Royal —
          And I trust ye are not she —
     Now tell me some of the love-tokens
          That past between you and me.'

13   'O dinna you mind now, Love Gregor,
          When we sat at the wine,
     How we changed the rings frae our fingers?
          And I can show thee thine.

14   'O yours was good, and good enneugh,
          But ay the best was mine;
     For yours was o the good red goud,
          But mine o the dimonds fine.

15   'But open the door now, Love Gregor,
          O open the door I pray,
     For your young son that is in my arms
          Will be dead ere it be day.'

16   'Awa, awa, ye ill woman,
          For here ye shanno win in;
     Gae drown ye in the raging sea,
          Or hang on the gallows-pin.'

17   When the cock had crawn, and day did dawn,
          And the sun began to peep,
     Then it raise him Love Gregor,
          And sair, sair did he weep.

18   'O I dreamd a dream, my mother dear,
          The thoughts o it gars me greet,
     That Fair Annie of Rough Royal
          Lay cauld dead at my feet.'

13 mind *remember*
16 win in *make your way in* · gallows-pin *gallows beam*

19 'Gin it be for Annie of Rough Royal
    That ye make a' this din,
She stood a' last night at this door,
    But I trow she wan no in.'

20 'O wae betide ye, ill woman,
    An ill dead may ye die!
That ye woudno open the door to her,
    Nor yet woud waken me.'

21 O he has gone down to yon shore-side,
    As fast as he could fare;
He saw Fair Annie in her boat,
    But the wind it tossd her sair.

22 And 'Hey, Annie!' and 'How, Annie!
    O Annie, winna ye bide?'
But ay the mair that he cried Annie,
    The braider grew the tide.

23 And 'Hey, Annie!' and 'How, Annie!
    Dear Annie, speak to me!'
But ay the louder he cried Annie,
    The louder roard the sea.

24 The wind blew loud, the sea grew rough,
    And dashd the boat on shore;
Fair Annie floats on the raging sea,
    But her young son raise no more.

25 Love Gregor tare his yellow hair,
    And made a heavy moan;
Fair Annie's corpse lay at his feet,
    But his bonny young son was gone.

19 trow *am sure* · 20 dead *death*

26 O cherry, cherry was her cheek,
    And gowden was her hair,
But clay cold were her rosey lips,
    Nae spark of life was there.

27 And first he's kissd her cherry cheek,
    And neist he's kissed her chin;
And saftly pressd her rosey lips,
    But there was nae breath within.

28 'O wae betide my cruel mother,
    And an ill dead may she die!
For she turnd my true-love frae my door,
    When she came sae far to me.'

59

The Drowned Lovers

1 Willie stands in his stable-door,
    And clapping at his steed,
And looking oer his white fingers
    His nose began to bleed.

2 'Gie corn to my horse, mother,
    And meat to my young man,
And I'll awa to Maggie's bower;
    I'll win ere she lie down.'

3 'O bide this night wi me, Willie,
    O bide this night wi me;
The best an cock o a' the reest
    At your supper shall be.'

1 clapping *patting*
2 meat *food* · win *get there*
3 reest *roost*

4 'A' your cocks, and a' your reests,
        I value not a prin,
   For I'll awa to Meggie's bower;
        I'll win ere she lie down.'

5 'Stay this night wi me, Willie,
        O stay this night wi me;
   The best an sheep in a' the flock
        At your supper shall be.'

6 'A' your sheep, and a' your flocks,
        I value not a prin,
   For I'll awa to Meggie's bower;
        I'll win ere she lie down.'

7 'O an ye gang to Meggie's bower,
        Sae sair against my will,
   The deepest pot in Clyde's water,
        My malison ye's feel.'

8 'The guid steed that I ride upon
        Cost me thrice thretty pound;
   And I'll put trust in his swift feet
        To hae me safe to land.'

9 As he rade ower yon high, high hill,
        And down yon dowie den,
   The noise that was in Clyde's water
        Woud feard five huner men.

10 'O roaring Clyde, ye roar ower loud,
        Your streams seem wondrous strang;
   Make me your wreck as I come back,
        But spare me as I gang!'

4 prin *pin*
7 pot *pool* · malison *curse*
9 dowie *gloomy, sad* · feard *frightened*

11 Then he is on to Maggie's bower,
        And tirled at the pin;
    'O sleep ye, wake ye, Meggie,' he said,
        'Ye'll open, lat me come in.'

12 'O wha is this at my bower-door,
        That calls me by my name?'
    'It is your first love, sweet Willie,
        This night newly come hame.'

13 'I hae few lovers thereout, thereout,
        As few hae I therein;
    The best an love that ever I had
        Was here just late yestreen.'

14 'The warstan stable in a' your stables,
        For my puir steed to stand!
    The warstan bower in a' your bowers,
        For me to lie therein!
    My boots are fu o Clyde's water,
        I'm shivering at the chin.'

15 'My barns are fu o corn, Willie,
        My stables are fu o hay;
    My bowers are fu o gentlemen,
        They'll nae remove till day.'

16 'O fare ye well, my fause Meggie,
        O farewell, and adieu!
    I've gotten my mither's malison
        This night coming to you.'

17 As he rode ower yon high, high hill,
        And down yon dowie den,
    The rushing that was in Clyde's water
        Took Willie's cane frae him.

18 He leand him ower his saddle-bow,
        To catch his cane again;
    The rushing that was in Clyde's water
        Took Willie's hat frae him.

19 He leand him ower his saddle-bow,
        To catch his hat thro force;
    The rushing that was in Clyde's water
        Took Willie frae his horse.

20 His brither stood upo the bank,
        Says, Fye, man, will ye drown?
    Ye'll turn ye to your high horse head
        And learn how to sowm.

21 'How can I turn to my horse head
        And learn how to sowm?
    I've gotten my mither's malison,
        It's here that I maun drown.'

22 The very hour this young man sank
        Into the pot sae deep,
    Up it wakend his love Meggie
        Out o her drowsy sleep.

23 'Come here, come here, my mither dear,
        And read this dreary dream;
    I dreamd my love was at our gates,
        And nane wad let him in.'

24 'Lye still, lye still now, my Meggie,
        Lye still and tak your rest;
    Sin your true-love was at your yates,
        It's but twa quarters past.'

20 sowm *swim*
23 dreary *ill-omened*
24 twa quarters *half-an-hour*

25 Nimbly, nimbly raise she up,
      And nimbly pat she on,
    And the higher that the lady cried,
      The louder blew the win.

26 The first an step that she steppd in,
      She stepped to the queet;
    'Ohon, alas!' said that lady,
      'This water's wondrous deep.'

27 The next an step that she wade in,
      She wadit to the knee;
    Says she, 'I coud wide farther in,
      If I my love coud see.'

28 The next an step that she wade in,
      She wadit to the chin;
    The deepest pot in Clyde's water
      She got sweet Willie in.

29 'You've had a cruel mither, Willie,
      And I have had anither;
    But we shall sleep in Clyde's water
      Like sister an like brither.'

25 pat she on *she dressed*
26 queet *ankle* · 27 wide *wade*

60

The Dowie Dens o' Yarrow

1 There was a layde lived in the North,
   Her name it was called Sara,
 She was coorted by nine noblemen,
   And a plooman lad frae Yarrow.

2 As he gaed owre yon hill sae high
   An' doon yon den sae narrow
 'Twas there he met nine armèd men
   Come to fecht wi' him in Yarrow.

3 Noo ye are a' come to fecht wi' me
   In the dowie dens o' Yarrow
 But there's nine o' you and but ane o' me
   An' its's nae an equal marrow.

4 There's nine o' you an' but ane o' me
   An' it's nae an equal marrow
 But I will fecht ye, ane by ane
   In the dowie dens o' Yarrow.

5 Three he slew, and three withdrew
   And three lay deadly wounded
 But in behind cam' her brother George
   An' pierced his body thorough.

6 Noo ye'll gang hame my cruel freen
   An' tell your sister Sara
 That her true love John lies dead and gone
   In the dowie dens o' Yarrow.

7 O mither dear I ha'e dreamed a dream
   An' I wish't may prove nae sorrow
 I dreamed I pu'd the heather bell
   On the bonnie braes o' Yarrow.

TITLE dowie *gloomy, sad*
2 den *small valley* · 3 marrow *match*

8 O daughter dear I can read your dream
    But I fear it will prove sorrow
For your true love John lies dead an' gone
    In the dowie dens o' Yarrow.

9 As she gaed owre yon hill sae high
    An' doon yon den sae narrow
'Twas there she spied her true love John
    A bloody corpse in Yarrow.

10 She wash'd his face and kemm'd his hair
    As aft she'd dune afore O
An' she washed the reed blude frae his wounds
    Wi' muckle grief and sorrow.

11 Her hair it was three quarters lang
    An' the colour o' it was yallow
She's tied it roon his middle sae sma'
    An' carried him hame frae Yarrow.

12 O daughter dear dry up your tears
    Dry up your tears o' sorrow
An' I'll find to you some prettier man
    Than the lad ye lost in Yarrow.

13 O ye may tak' your seven sons
    An' wed them all tomorrow
But a fairer flower ne'er sprang in June
    Than the lad I lost in Yarrow.

14 O mither dear ye'll mak' my bed
    Ye'll mak' it saft an' narrow
An' there I'll lie an' thus I'll die
    For the lad I lost in Yarrow.

11 three quarters *three quarters of a yard*

15 Her mither then did mak' her bed
　　She made it saft an' narrow
An' her tender heart it soon did break
　　An' she died afore 'twas morrow.

61

The Douglas Tragedy

1 'Rise up, rise up, now, Lord Douglas,' she says,
　　'And put on your armour so bright;
Let it never be said that a daughter of thine
　　Was married to a lord under night.

2 'Rise up, rise up, my seven bold sons,
　　And put on your armour so bright,
And take better care of your youngest sister,
　　For your eldest's awa the last night.'

3 He's mounted her on a milk-white steed,
　　And himself on a dapple grey,
With a bugelet horn hung down by his side,
　　And lightly they rode away.

4 Lord William lookit oer his left shoulder,
　　To see what he could see,
And there he spy'd her seven brethren bold,
　　Come riding over the lee.

5 'Light down, light down, Lady Margret,' he said,
　　'And hold my steed in your hand,
Until that against your seven brethren bold,
　　And your father, I mak a stand.'

3 bugelet *bugle* · 4 lee *grass land*

6 She held his steed in her milk-white hand,
    And never shed one tear,
Until that she saw her seven brethren fa,
    And her father hard fighting, who lovd her so dear.

7 'O hold your hand, Lord William!' she said,
    'For your strokes they are wondrous sair;
True lovers I can get many a ane,
    But a father I can never get mair.'

8 O she's taen out her handkerchief,
    It was o the holland sae fine,
And aye she dighted her father's bloody wounds,
    That were redder than the wine.

9 'O chuse, O chuse, Lady Margret,' he said,
    'O whether will ye gang or bide?'
'I'll gang, I'll gang, Lord William,' she said,
    'For ye have left me no other guide.'

10 He's lifted her on a milk-white steed,
    And himself on a dapple grey,
With a bugelet horn hung down by his side,
    And slowly they baith rade away.

11 O they rade on, and on they rade,
    And a' by the light of the moon,
Until they came to yon wan water,
    And there they lighted down.

12 They lighted down to tak a drink
    Of the spring that ran sae clear,
And down the stream ran his gude heart's blood,
    And sair she gan to fear.

8 holland *linen* · dighted *wiped*

13 'Hold up, hold up, Lord William,' she says,
    'For I fear that you are slain;'
    ''T is naething but the shadow of my scarlet cloak,
    That shines in the water sae plain.'

14 O they rade on, and on they rade,
    And a' by the light of the moon,
    Until they cam to his mother's ha door,
    And there they lighted down.

15 'Get up, get up, lady mother,' he says,
    'Get up, and let me in!
    Get up, get up, lady mother,' he says,
    'For this night my fair lady I've win.

16 'O mak my bed, lady mother,' he says,
    'O mak it braid and deep,
    And lay Lady Margret close at my back,
    And the sounder I will sleep.'

17 Lord William was dead lang ere midnight,
    Lady Margret lang ere day,
    And all true lovers that go thegither,
    May they have mair luck than they!

18 Lord William was buried in St. Mary's kirk,
    Lady Margret in Mary's quire;
    Out o the lady's grave grew a bonny red rose,
    And out o the knight's a briar.

19 And they twa met, and they twa plat,
    And fain they wad be near;
    And a' the warld might ken right weel
    They were twa lovers dear.

18 quire *choir*
19 plat *pleated together*

20 But bye and rade the Black Douglas,
  And wow but he was rough!
For he pulld up the bonny brier,
  And flang't in St. Mary's Loch.

62

Clerk Sanders

1 Clark Sanders and May Margret
  Walkt ower yon graveld green,
And sad and heavy was the love,
  I wat, it fell this twa between.

2 'A bed, a bed,' Clark Sanders said,
  'A bed, a bed for you and I;'
'Fye no, fye no,' the lady said,
  'Until the day we married be.

3 'For in it will come my seven brothers,
  And a' their torches burning bright;
They'll say, We hae but ae sister,
  And here her lying wi a knight.'

4 'Ye'l take the sourde fray my scabbord,
  And lowly, lowly lift the gin,
And you may say, your oth to save,
  You never let Clark Sanders in.

5 'Yele take a napken in your hand,
  And ye'l ty up baith your een,
An ye may say, your oth to save,
  That ye saw na Sandy sen late yestreen.

1 graveld green *gravelly grass* · it fell *that fell*
4 sourde *sword* · lowly *quietly* · gin *latch*

6 'Yele take me in your armes twa,
    Yele carrey me ben into your bed,
And ye may say, your oth to save,
    In your bower-floor I never tread.'

7 She has taen the sourde fray his scabbord,
    And lowly, lowly lifted the gin;
She was to swear, her oth to save,
    She never let Clerk Sanders in.

8 She has tain a napkin in her hand,
    And she ty'd up baith her eeen;
She was to swear, her oth to save,
    She saw na him sene late yestreen.

9 She has taen him in her armes twa,
    And carried him ben into her bed;
She was to swear, her oth to save,
    He never in her bower-floor tread.

10 In and came her seven brothers,
    And all their torches burning bright;
Says thay, We hae but ae sister,
    And see there her lying wi a knight.

11 Out and speaks the first of them,
    'A wat they hay been lovers dear;'
Out and speaks the next of them,
    'They hay been in love this many a year.'

12 Out an speaks the third of them,
    'It wear great sin this twa to twain;'
Out an speaks the fourth of them,
    'It wear a sin to kill a sleeping man.'

6 ben *in* · 8 sene *since*
12 sin *shame* · twain *separate*

13 Out an speaks the fifth of them,
     'A wat they'll near be twaind by me;'
  Out an speaks the sixt of them,
     'We'l tak our leave an gae our way.'

14 Out an speaks the seventh of them,
     'Altho there wear no a man but me,
   . . . .
     I bear the brand, I'le gar him die.'

15 Out he has taen a bright long brand,
     And he has striped it throw the straw,
  And throw and throw Clarke Sanders' body
     A wat he has gard cold iron gae.

16 Sanders he started, an Margret she lapt,
     Intill his arms whare she lay,
  And well and wellsom was the night,
     A wat it was between these twa.

17 And they lay still, and sleeped sound,
     Untill the day began to daw;
  And kindly till him she did say
     'It's time, trew-love, ye wear awa.'

18 They lay still, and sleeped sound,
     Untill the sun began to shine;
  She lookt between her and the wa,
     And dull and heavy was his eeen.

19 She thought it had been a loathsome sweat,
     A wat it had fallen this twa between;
  But it was the blood of his fair body,
     A wat his life days wair na lang.

15 striped it *whetted it by slashing it* · straw *bed-straw*
17 daw *dawn*
19 it had fallen *that had fallen*

20 'O Sanders, I'le do for your sake
  What other ladys would na thoule;
When seven years is come and gone,
  There's near a shoe go on my sole.

21 'O Sanders, I'le do for your sake
  What other ladies would think mare;
When seven years is come an gone,
  Ther's nere a comb go in my hair.

22 'O Sanders, I'le do for your sake
  What other ladies would think lack;
When seven years is come an gone,
  I'le wear nought but dowy black.'

23 The bells gaed clinking throw the towne,
  To carry the dead corps to the clay,
An sighing says her May Margret,
  'A wat I bide a doulfou day.'

24 In an come her father dear,
  Stout steping on the floor;
  . . . .
  . . . .

25 'Hold your toung, my doughter dear,
  Let all your mourning a bee;
I'le carry the dead corps to the clay,
  An I'le come back an comfort thee.'

26 'Comfort well your seven sons,
  For comforted will I never bee;
For it was neither lord nor loune
  That was in bower last night wi mee.'

20 thoule *endure* · 22 dowy *sad*
23 doulfou *doleful*
26 loune *man of low rank*

63

Lady Maisry

1 The young lords o the north country
  Have all a wooing gone,
To win the love of Lady Maisry,
  But o them she woud hae none.

2 O they hae courted Lady Maisry
  Wi a' kin kind of things;
An they hae sought her Lady Maisry
  Wi brotches an wi' rings.

3 An they ha sought her Lady Maisry
  Frae father and frae mother;
An they ha sought her Lady Maisry
  Frae sister an frae brother.

4 An they ha followd her Lady Maisry
  Thro chamber an thro ha;
But a' that they coud say to her,
  Her answer still was Na.

5 'O had your tongues, young men,' she says,
  'An think nae mair o me;
For I've gien my love to an English lord,
  An think nae mair o me.'

6 Her father's kitchy-boy heard that,
  An ill death may he dee!
An he is on to her brother,
  As fast as gang coud he.

7 'O is my father an my mother well,
  But an my brothers three?
Gin my sister Lady Maisry be well,
  There's naething can ail me.'

2 a' kin kind *every kind*
7 but an *and also*

8 'Your father and your mother is well,
        But an your brothers three;
    Your sister Lady Maisry's well,
        So big wi bairn gangs she.'

9 'Gin this be true you tell to me,
        My mailison light on thee!
    But gin it be a lie you tell,
        You sal be hangit hie.'

10 He's done him to his sister's bowr,
        Wi meikle doole an care;
    An there he saw her Lady Maisry,
        Kembing her yallow hair.

11 'O wha is aught that bairn,' he says,
        'That ye sae big are wi?
    And gin ye winna own the truth,
        This moment ye sall dee.'

12 She turnd her right an roun about,
        An the kem fell frae her han;
    A trembling seizd her fair body,
        An her rosy cheek grew wan.

13 'O pardon me, my brother dear,
        An the truth I'll tell to thee;
    My bairn it is to Lord William,
        An he is betrothd to me.'

14 'O coud na ye gotten dukes, or lords,
        Intill your ain country,
    That ye draw up wi an English dog,
        To bring this shame on me?

9 mailison *curse*
10 doole *grief*
11 wha is aught *whose is*
14 draw up *take up*

15 'But ye maun gi up the English lord,
        Whan youre young babe is born;
    For, gin you keep by him an hour langer,
        Your life sall be forlorn.'

16 'I will gi up this English blood,
        Till my young babe be born;
    But the never a day nor hour langer,
        Tho my life should be forlorn.'

17 'O whare is a' my merry young men,
        Whom I gi meat and fee,
    To pu the thistle and the thorn,
        To burn this wile whore wi?'

18 'O whare will I get a bonny boy,
        To help me in my need,
    To rin wi hast to Lord William,
        And bid him come wi speed?'

19 O out it spake a bonny boy,
        Stood by her brother's side:
    'O I would rin your errand, lady,
        Oer a' the world wide.

20 'Aft have I run your errands, lady,
        Whan blawn baith win and weet;
    But now I'll rin your errand, lady,
        Wi sat tears on my cheek.'

21 O whan he came to broken briggs,
        He bent his bow and swam,
    An whan he came to the green grass growin,
        He slackd his shoone and ran.

15 forlorn *lost*
17 wile *vile*
21 briggs *bridges*

22 O whan he came to Lord William's gates,
    He baed na to chap or ca,
But set his bent bow till his breast,
    An lightly lap the wa;
An, or the porter was at the gate,
    The boy was i the ha.

23 'O is my biggins broken, boy?
    Or is my towers won?
Or is my lady lighter yet,
    Of a dear daughter or son?'

24 'Your biggin is na broken, sir,
    Nor is your towers won;
But the fairest lady in a' the lan
    For you this day maun burn.'

25 'O saddle me the black, the black,
    Or saddle me the brown;
O saddle me the swiftest steed
    That ever rade frae a town.'

26 Or he was near a mile awa,
    She heard his wild horse sneeze:
'Mend up the fire, my false brother,
    It's na come to my knees.'

27 O whan he lighted at the gate,
    She heard his bridle ring:
'Mend up the fire, my false brother,
    It's far yet frae my chin.

28 'Mend up the fire to me, brother,
    Mend up the fire to me;
For I see him comin hard an fast
    Will soon men't up to thee.

22 baed *waited* · chap *knock* · lap *leapt* · or *before*
23 biggins *buildings*

29 'O gin my hands had been loose, Willy,
    Sae hard as they are boun,
I would have turnd me frae the gleed,
    And castin out your young son.'

30 'O I'll gar burn for you, Maisry,
    Your father an your mother;
An I'll gar burn for you, Maisry,
    Your sister an your brother.

31 'An I'll gar burn for you, Maisry,
    The chief of a' your kin;
An the last bonfire that I come to,
    Mysel I will cast in.'

29 gleed *fire*

64

The Broom o the Cathery Knowes

1 'It's hold your hand, dear judge,' she says,
    'O hold your hand for a while!
For yonder I see my father a coming,
    Riding many's the mile.

2 'Have you any gold, father?' she says,
    'Or have you any fee?
Or did you come to see your own daughter a hanging,
    Like a dog, upon a tree?'

3 'I have no gold, daughter,' he says,
    'Neither have I any fee;
But I am come to see my ain daughter hanged,
    And hanged she shall be.'

2 fee *possessions, wealth* · tree *gallows*

4 'Hey the broom, and the bonny, bonny broom,
     The broom o the Cauthery Knowes!
  I wish I were at hame again,
     Milking my ain daddie's ewes.

5 'Hold your hand, dear judge,' she says,
     'O hold your hand for a while!
  For yonder I see my own mother coming,
     Riding full many a mile.

6 'Have you any gold, mother?' she says,
     'Or have you any fee?
  Or did you come to see your own daughter hanged,
     Like a dog, upon a tree?'

7 'I have no gold, daughter,' she says,
     'Neither have I any fee;
  But I am come to see my own daughter hanged,
     And hanged she shall be.'

8 'Hey the broom, the bonnie, bonnie broom,
     The broom o the Cauthery Knowes!
  I wish I were at hame again,
     Milking my ain daddie's ewes.

9 'Hold your hand, dear judge,' she says,
     'O hold your hand for a while!
  For yonder I see my ae brother a coming,
     Riding many's the mile.

10 'Have you any gold, brother?' she says,
     'Or have you any fee?
  Or did you come to see your ain sister a hanging,
     Like a dog, upon a tree?'

11 'I have no gold, sister,' she says,
     'Nor have I any fee;
  But I am come to see my ain sister hanged,
     And hanged she shall be.'

12 'Hey the broom, the bonnie, bonnie broom,
    The broom o the Cathery Knowes!
I wish I were at hame again,
    Milking my ain daddie's ewes.

13 'Hold your hand, dear judge,' she says,
    'O hold your hand for a while!
For yonder I see my own true-love coming,
    Riding full many a mile.

14 'Have you any gold, my true-love?' she says,
    'Or have you any fee?
Or have you come to see your own love hanged,
    Like a dog, upon a tree?'

* * * * *

65

The Cruel Brother

1 A gentleman cam oure the sea,
    Fine flowers in the valley
And he has courted ladies three.
    With the light green and the yellow

2 One o them was clad in red:
He asked if she wad be his bride.

3 One o them was clad in green:
He asked if she wad be his queen.

4 The last o them was clad in white:
He asked if she wad be his heart's delight.

5 'Ye may ga ask my father, the king:
Sae maun ye ask my mither, the queen.

6 'Sae maun ye ask my sister Anne:
   And dinna forget my brither John.'

7 He has asked her father, the king:
   And sae did he her mither, the queen.

8 And he has asked her sister Anne:
   But he has forgot her brother John.

9 Her father led her through the ha,
   Her mither danced afore them a'.

10 Her sister Anne led her through the closs,
   Her brither John set her on her horse.

11 It's then he drew a little penknife,
   And he reft the fair maid o her life.

12 'Ride up, ride up,' said the foremost man;
   'I think our bride comes hooly on.'

13 'Ride up, ride up,' said the second man;
   'I think our bride looks pale and wan.'

14 Up than cam the gay bridegroom,
   And straucht unto the bride he cam.

15 'Does your side-saddle sit awry?
   Or does you steed . . . .

16 'Or does the rain run in your glove?
   Or wad ye chuse anither love?'

17 'The rain runs not in my glove,
   Nor will I e'er chuse anither love.
      10 closs *courtyard*
      12 hooly *slowly, softly*

18 'But O an I war at Saint Evron's well,
    There I wad licht, and drink my fill!

19 'Oh an I war at Saint Evron's closs,
    There I wad licht, and bait my horse!'

20 Whan she cam to Saint Evron's well,
    She dought na licht to drink her fill.

21 Whan she cam to Saint Evron's closs,
    The bonny bride fell aff her horse.

22 'What will ye leave to your father, the king?'
    'The milk-white steed that I ride on.'

23 'What will ye leave to your mother, the queen?'
    'The bluidy robes that I have on.'

24 'What will ye leave to your sister Anne?'
    'My gude lord, to be wedded on.'

25 'What will ye leave to your brither John?'
    'The gallows pin to hang him on.'

26 'What will ye leave to your brither's wife?'
    'Grief and sorrow a' the days o her life.'

27 'What will ye leave to your brither's bairns?'
    'The meal-pock to hang oure the arms.'

28 Now does she neither sigh nor groan:
    She lies aneath yon marble stone.

19 bait *feed*
20 dought *could*
25 gallows pin *gallows beam*
27 meal-pock *beggar's meal bag*

66

Son David

1 'Oh, what's the blood 'it's on your sword,
    My son David, ho, son David?
  What's that blood 'it's on your sword?
    Come, promise, tell me true.'

2 'Oh, that's the blood of my grey meer,
    Hey, lady Mother, ho, lady Mother,
  That's the blood of my grey meer,
    Because it wadnae rule by me.'

3 'Oh, that blood it is owre clear,
    My son David, ho, son David,
  That blood it is owre clear,
    Come, promise, tell me true.'

4 'Oh, that's the blood of my greyhound,
    Hey, lady Mother, ho, lady Mother,
  That's the blood of my greyhound,
    Because it wadnae rule by me.'

5 'Oh, that blood it is owre clear,
    My son David, ho, son David,
  That blood it is owre clear,
    Come, promise, tell me true.'

6 'Oh, that's the blood of my huntin hawk,
    Hey, lady Mother, ho, lady Mother,
  That's the blood of my huntin hawk,
    Because it wadnae rule by me.'

7 'Oh, that blood it is owre clear,
    My son David, ho, son David,
  That blood it is owre clear,
    Come, promise, tell me true.'

2 meer *mare*

8   'For that's the blood of my brother John,
        Hey, lady Mother, ho, lady Mother,
     That's the blood of my brother John,
        Because he wadnae rule by me.'

9   'Oh, I'm gaun awa in a bottomless boat,
        In a bottomless boat, in a bottomless boat,
     For I'm gaun awa in a bottomless boat,
        An I'll never return again.'

10 'Oh, whan will you come back again,
        My son David, ho, son David?
     Whan will you come back again?
        Come, promise, tell me true.'

11 'When the sun an the moon meet in yon glen,
        Hey, lady Mother, ho, lady Mother,
     When the sun an the moon meet in yon glen,
        For I'll return again.'

67

Rosianne

1   Rosie she sat in her simmer bour
        Weeping an makand grit mane
     Whan doun by cam her faither
        Sayand what ails thee Rosianne

2   A deal a deal deir father she said
        Grit reason hae I to mane
     For thare lyes a little babe in my syde
        Between me an my brither John

3 Rosie she sat in her simmer bour
      Weeping an makand a grit mane
   Wha cam by but her mither deir
      Sayand what ails thee Rosianne

4 A deal a deal deir mither she said
      Grit reason hae I to mane
   For thare lyes a little babe in my side
      Between me an my brither John

5 Rosie she sat in her simmer bour
      Weeping an makan grit mane
   Wha cam doun but her sister deir
      Sayand what ails thee Rosianne

6 A deal a deal deir sister she said
      Grit reason hae I to mane
   For there lies a little babe in my side
      Between me and my brither John

7 Rosie she sat in her simmer bowr
      Weeping an makand grit mane
   Wha cam by but her fause fause brither
      Sayand what ails thee Rosianne

8 A deal a deal deir brither she said
      Grit reason hae I to mane
   For there lies a little babe in my side
      Between me an thee, deir brither John.

9 Weil ye hae tauld faither an ye hae tauld mither
      And ye hae tauld sister aw thrie
   Syne he pou't out his wee penknyfe
      An gae her deep wounds three

8 a deal *a great deal*

10 What blude is that on the point of your knyfe
      Deir son cum tell to me
   It is my horse's that I hae killit
      Deir mither and fair ladie

11 The blude o your horse was neir sae red
      Deir son cum tell to me
   It is my grandfather's that I hae killit
      Dear mither and fair ladie

12 The blude o your grandfather was neir sae free
      Dear son cum tell to me
   It is my sister's that I hae killit
      Dear mither and fair ladie

13 What will ye do whan your father cums hame
      Dear son cum tell to me
   I'll set my fit on yon ship bord
      An I howp she'll sail wi me

14 What will ye do wi your bonnie wife
      Deir son cum tell to me
   I'll set her in anither ship
      And I howp she'll fallow me

15 An' what will ye do wi' your little son
      Dear son come tell tae me
   I'll lea' him wi' you my dearest mither
      Tae keep ye in mind o' me

16 What will ye do wi' your houses an' lan'
      Dear son com tell tae me
   I'll lea' them wi' you dear mither
      Tae maintain my wee babie

12 free *fine*
15 keep ye in mind *remind you*

17 An whan will you return again
      Dear son come tell tae me
  Whan the Sun an' Moon meet on yon hill
      An' I hope that will never be

68

Lady Jean

1 The King's young dochter was sittan in her window
      Sewan at hir fine silken seam
  Sho luikit out at her braw bower window
      And she saw the leaves growan grein my love
      And she saw the leaves growan grein

2 She stack her neidle into her sleive
      Her seam down by her tae
  And she is awa to the merrie green wud
      For to pu the nuts and slaes

3 She had na pu't a nit at aw
      A nit but scarcely three
  Till out and spak a braw young man
      Saying how daurst thou bow this tree

4 It's I will pu these nuts she said
      An I will bow this tree
  An I will come to the merrie grein wud
      An no ask leave of thee

5 He tuke her be the middle sae smaw
      And laid her on the gerse sae green
  An he has tane his will of her
      An he luit her up again

2 slaes *sloes*
5 gerse *grass*

6 Now since you have got your will o me
        Pray tell to me your name
   For I am the King's young dochter she said
        And this nicht I daur na gang hame

7 If ye be the King's young dochter he said
        I am his auldest son
   I wish I had died on some distant isle
        An never had come hame

8 The first time I came hame Jeinie
        Thow was na here nor born
   I wish my prettie ship had sunk
        An I had neir returned

9 The neist time I cam hame Jeanie
        Thou was sittan on the nurse's knie
   An I wiss my pretty ship had sunk
        An I had seen neir thee

10 An the neist time I came hame Jeinie
        I met thee here alane
   I wiss I had die't on some distant isle
        An never had come hame

11 She put her hand down by her side
        Doun into her spare
   An she pu't out a wee pen knife
        An she woundit hersel fu sair

12 Slowlie, slowlie, rose she up
        An slowlie she gade hame
   Until she cam to her faither's parlour
        And there she did sigh and mane

9 neist *next*
11 spare *opening in her gown*

13 O Sister Sister mak my bed
     O' the clean sheets and strae
  O Sister sister mak my bed
     Down in the parlour below

14 And her faither he came trippan down the stairs
     His steps they were fu slow
  I think, I think, ladie Jean he said
     Ye'r lyan far owr low

15 O late last night as I came hame
     Down by yon castle wa
  O heavy heavy was the stane
     That on my breast did faw

16 Her mother she came doun the stair
     Her steps they were fu slow
  I think I think lady Jean she said
     Ye'r lyan far owr low

17 O late last night as I came hame
     Down by yon castle wa
  O heavy heavy was the stane
     That on my breast did faw

18 Her Sister came tripping doun the stair
     Her steps they were fu slow
  I think I think lady Jean she said
     Ye're lying far ower low

19 O late last night as I came hame
     Down by yon castle wa
  O heavy heavy was the stane
     That on my breast did faw

13 strae *straw*

20 Her brither he came trippan doun the stair
    His steps they were fu slow
He sank into his sister's arms
    And they died as white as snow

69

The Broom Blooms Bonnie and Says It Is Fair

1 It is talked the warld all over,
    The brume blooms bonnie and says it is fair
That the king's dochter gaes wi child to her brither.
    And we'll never gang doun to the brume onie mair

2 He's taen his sister doun to her father's deer park,
    Wi his yew-tree bow and arrows fast slung to his back.

3 'Now when that ye hear me gie a loud cry,
    Shoot frae thy bow an arrow and there let me lye.

4 'And when that ye see I am lying dead,
    Then ye'll put me in a grave, wi a turf at my head.'

5 Now when he heard her gie a loud cry,
    His silver arrow frae his bow he suddenly let fly.
        Now they'll never, etc.

6 He has made a grave that was lang and was deep,
    And he has buried his sister, wi her babe at her feet.
        And they'll never, etc.

7 And when he came to his father's court hall,
    There was music and minstrels and dancing and all.
        But they'll never, etc.

8　'O Willie, O Willie, what makes thee in pain?'
　　'I have lost a sheath and knife that I'll never see again.'
　　　　For we'll never, etc.

9　'There is ships o your father's sailing on the sea
　　That will bring as good a sheath and a knife unto thee.'

10　'There is ships o my father's sailing on the sea,
　　But sic a sheath and a knife they can never bring to me.'
　　　　Now we'll never, etc.

70

The High Banks o Yarrow

1　Down in Dumbarton there wonnd a rich merchant,
　　Down in Dumbarton there wond a rich merchant,
　　And he had nae family but ae only dochter.
　　　　Sing fal lal de deedle, fal lal de deedle lair, O a day

2　There cam a rich squire, intending to woo her,
　　He wooed her until he had got her wi babie.

3　'Oh what shall I do! oh what shall come o me!
　　Baith father and mither will think naething o me.'

4　'Gae up your father, bring down gowd and money,
　　And I'll take ye ower to a braw Irish ladie.'

5　She gade to her father, brought down gowd and money,
　　And she's awa ower to a braw Irish ladie.

6　She hadna sailed far till the young thing cried 'Women!'
　　'What women can do, my dear, I'll do for you.'

1 wonnd *lived*

[237]

7 'O haud your tongue, foolish man, dinna talk vainly,
   For ye never kent what a woman driet for you.

8 'Gae wash your hands in the cauld spring water,
   And dry them on a towel a' giltit wi silver.

9 'And tak me by the middle, and lift me up saftlie,
   And throw me ower shipboard, baith me and my babie.'

10 He took her by the middle, and lifted her saftly,
   And threw her ower shipboard, baith her and her babie.

11 Sometimes she did sink, sometimes she did float it,
   Until that she cam to the high banks o Yarrow.

12 'O captain tak gowd, O sailors tak money,
   And launch out your sma boat till I sail for my honey.'

13 'How can I tak gowd, how can I tak money?
   My ship's on a sand bank, she winna sail for me.'

14 The captain took gowd, the sailors took money,
   And they launchd out their sma boat till he sailed for his honey.

15 'Mak my love a coffin o the gowd sae yellow,
   Whar the wood it is dear, and the planks they are narrow,
   And bury my love on the high banks o Yarrow.'

16 They made her a coffin o the gowd sae yellow,
   And buried her deep on the high banks o Yarrow.

7 driet *suffered* · 8 giltit *ornamented*
9 ower shipboard *overboard*

71

Willie's Lady

1 Willie has taen him oer the fame,
　He's woo'd a wife and brought her hame.

2 He's woo'd her for her yellow hair,
　But his mother wrought her mickle care.

3 And mickle dolour gard her dree,
　For lighter she can never be.

4 But in her bower she sits wi pain,
　And Willie mourns oer her in vain.

5 And to his mother he has gone,
　That vile rank witch of vilest kind.

6 He says: 'My ladie has a cup,
　Wi gowd and silver set about.

7 'This goodlie gift shall be your ain,
　And let her be lighter o her young bairn.'

8 'Of her young bairn she'll neer be lighter,
　Nor in her bower to shine the brighter.

9 'But she shall die and turn to clay,
　And you shall wed another may.'

10 'Another may I'll never wed,
　Another may I'll neer bring home.'

11 But sighing says that weary wight,
　'I wish my life were at an end.'

　　　1 taen him *gone* · fame *foam, sea*
　　　3 dolour *grief* · dree *suffer* · lighter *delivered*
　　　9 may *maiden* · 11 wight *person*

12 'Ye doe [ye] unto your mother again,
  That vile rank witch of vilest kind.

13 'And say your ladie has a steed,
  The like o 'm 's no in the lands of Leed.

14 'For he [i]s golden shod before,
  And he [i]s golden shod behind.

15 'And at ilka tet of that horse's main,
  There's a golden chess and a bell ringing.

16 'This goodlie gift shall be your ain,
  And let me be lighter of my young bairn.'

17 'O her young bairn she'll neer be lighter,
  Nor in her bower to shine the brighter.

18 'But she shall die and turn to clay,
  And ye shall wed another may.'

19 'Another may I['ll] never wed,
  Another may I['ll] neer bring hame.'

20 But sighing said that weary wight,
  'I wish my life were at an end.'

21 'Ye doe [ye] unto your mother again,
  That vile rank witch of vilest kind.

22 'And say your ladie has a girdle,
  It's red gowd unto the middle.

23 'And ay at every silver hem,
  Hangs fifty silver bells and ten.

12 doe ye *go*
13 o 'm 's *of him is*
15 ilka tet *every lock* · chess *jess, strap*

24 'That goodlie gift shall be her ain,
   And let me be lighter of my young bairn.'

25 'O her young bairn she's neer be lighter,
   Nor in her bower to shine the brighter.

26 'But she shall die and turn to clay,
   And you shall wed another may.'

27 'Another may I'll never wed,
   Another may I'll neer bring hame.'

28 But sighing says that weary wight,
   'I wish my life were at an end.'

29 Then out and spake the Belly Blind;
   He spake aye in good time.

30 'Ye doe ye to the market place,
   And there ye buy a loaf o wax.

31 'Ye shape it bairn and bairnly like,
   And in twa glassen een ye pit;

32 'And bid her come to your boy's christening;
   Then notice weel what she shall do.

33 'And do you stand a little fore bye,
   And listen weel what she shall say.'

34 'Oh wha has loosed the nine witch knots
   That was amo that ladie's locks?

35 'And wha has taen out the kaims of care
   That hangs amo that ladie's hair?

29 Belly Blind *name of a household spirit*
30 loaf *cake*
33 a little fore bye *near by*

36 'And wha's taen down the bush o woodbine
   That hang atween her bower and mine?

37 'And wha has killd the master kid
   That ran beneath that ladie's bed?

38 'And wha has loosed her left-foot shee,
   And lotten that ladie lighter be?'

39 O Willie has loosed the nine witch knots
   That was amo that ladie's locks.

40 And Willie's taen out the kaims o care
   That hang amo that ladie's hair.

41 And Willie's taen down the bush o woodbine
   That hang atween her bower and thine.

42 And Willie has killed the master kid
   That ran beneath that ladie's bed.

43 And Willie has loosed her left-foot shee,
   And letten his ladie lighter be.

44 And now he's gotten a bonny young son,
   And mickle grace be him upon.

72

Lamkin

1 It's Lamkin was a mason good
      As ever built wi stane;
   He built Lord Wearie's castle,
      But payment got he nane.

2 'O pay me, Lord Wearie,
       Come, pay me my fee:'
   'I canna pay you, Lamkin,
       For I maun gang oer the sea.'

3 'O pay me now, Lord Wearie,
       Come, pay me out o hand:'
   'I canna pay you, Lamkin,
       Unless I sell my land.'

4 'O gin ye winna pay me,
       I here sall mak a vow,
   Before that ye come hame again,
       Ye sall hae cause to rue.'

5 Lord Wearie got a bonny ship,
       To sail the saut sea faem;
   Bade his lady weel the castle keep,
       Ay till he should come hame.

6 But the nourice was a fause limmer
       As eer hung on a tree;
   She laid a plot wi Lamkin,
       Whan her lord was oer the sea.

7 She laid a plot wi Lamkin,
       When the servants were awa,
   Loot him in at a little shot-window,
       And brought him to the ha.

8 'O whare's a' the men o this house,
       That ca me Lamkin?'
   'They're at the barn-well thrashing;
       'T will be lang ere they come in.'

3 out o hand *immediately*
6 nourice *nurse* · limmer *wretch* · tree *gallows*
7 shot-window *hinged window*

9 'And whare's the women o this house,
    That ca me Lamkin?'
'They're at the far well washing;
    'T will be lang ere they come in.'

10 'And whare's the bairns o this house,
    That ca me Lamkin?'
'They're at the school reading;
    'T will be night or they come hame.'

11 'O whare's the lady o this house,
    That ca's me Lamkin?'
'She's up in her bower sewing,
    But we soon can bring her down.'

12 Then Lamkin's tane a sharp knife,
    That hang down by his gaire,
And he has gien the bonny babe
    A deep wound and a sair.

13 Then Lamkin he rocked,
    And the fause nourice sang,
Till frae ilkae bore o the cradle
    The red blood out sprang.

14 Then out it spak the lady,
    As she stood on the stair:
'What ails my bairn, nourice,
    That he's greeting sae sair?

15 'O still my bairn, nourice,
    O still him wi the pap!'
'He winna still, lady,
    For this nor for that.'

12 gaire *part of garment by knee*
13 ilkae bore *every hole*

16 'O still my bairn, nourice,
       O still him wi the wand!'
   'He winna still, lady,
       For a' his father's land.'

17 'O still my bairn, nourice,
       O still him wi the bell!'
   'He winna still, lady,
       Till ye come down yoursel.'

18 O the firsten step she steppit,
       She steppit on a stane;
   But the neisten step she steppit,
       She met him Lamkin.

19 'O mercy, mercy, Lamkin,
       Hae mercy upon me!
   Though you've taen my young son's life,
       Ye may let mysel be.'

20 'O sall I kill her, nourice,
       Or sall I lat her be?'
   'O kill her, kill her, Lamkin,
       For she neer was good to me.'

21 'O scour the bason, nourice,
       And mak it fair and clean,
   For to keep this lady's heart's blood,
       For she's come o noble kin.'

22 'There need nae bason, Lamkin,
       Lat it run through the floor;
   What better is the heart's blood
       O the rich than o the poor?'

16 wand *stick*
18 neisten *next*

23 But ere three months were at an end,
    Lord Wearie came again;
But dowie, dowie was his heart
    When first he came hame.

24 'O wha's blood is this,' he says,
    'That lies in the chamer?'
'It is your lady's heart's blood;
    'T is as clear as the lamer.'

25 'And wha's blood is this,' he says,
    'That lies in my ha?'
'It is your young son's heart's blood;
    'T is the clearest ava.'

26 O sweetly sang the black-bird
    That sat upon the tree;
But sairer grat Lamkin,
    When he was condemnd to die.

27 And bonny sang the mavis,
    Out o the thorny brake;
But sairer grat the nourice,
    When she was tied to the stake.

23 dowie *sad*
24 chamer *chamber* · lamer *amber*
25 ava *of all*
27 mavis *thrush* · brake *thicket*

73

The Jew's Daughter

1 The rain rins doun through Mirry-land toune,
    Sae dois it doune the Pa;
Sae dois the lads of Mirry-land toune,
    Whan they play at the ba.

2 Than out and cam the Jewis dochter,
    Said, Will ye cum in and dine?
 'I winnae cum in, I cannae cum in,
    Without my play-feres nine.'

3 Scho powd an apple reid and white,
    To intice the yong thing in:
 Scho powd an apple white and reid,
    And that the sweit bairne did win.

4 And scho has taine out a little pen-knife,
    And low down by her gair;
 Scho has twin'd the yong thing and his life,
    A word he nevir spak mair.

5 And out and cam the thick, thick bluid,
    And out and cam the thin,
 And out and cam the bonny herts bluid;
    Thair was nae life left in.

6 Scho laid him on a dressing-borde,
    And drest him like a swine,
 And laughing said, Gae nou and pley
    With your sweit play-feres nine.

7 Scho rowd him in a cake of lead,
    Bade him lie stil and sleip;
 Scho cast him in a deip draw-well,
    Was fifty fadom deip.

8 Whan bells wer rung, and mass was sung,
    And every lady went hame,
 Than ilka lady had her yong sonne,
    Bot Lady Helen had nane.

2 play-feres *playmates* · 3 win *succeed in enticing*
4 twin'd *separated*
6 dressing-borde *board for preparing food*
7 rowd *wrapped* · cake *sheet* · draw-well *deep well
from which water is drawn by a bucket on a rope*

9 Scho rowd hir mantil hir about,
      And sair, sair gan she weip,
  And she ran into the Jewis castel,
      Whan they wer all asleip.

10 'My bonny Sir Hew, my pretty Sir Hew,
      I pray thee to me speik:'
  'O lady, rinn to the deip draw-well,
      Gin ye your sonne wad seik.'

11 Lady Helen ran to the deip draw-well,
      And knelt upon her kne:
  'My bonny Sir Hew, an ye be here,
      I pray thee speik to me.'

12 'The lead is wondrous heavy, mither,
      The well is wondrous deip;
  A keen pen-knife sticks in my hert,
      A word I dounae speik.

13 'Gae hame, gae hame, my mither deir,
      Fetch me my windling sheet,
  And at the back o Mirry-land toun,
      It's thair we twa sall meet.'

9 gan she weip *she began to weep*
12 dounae *cannot*
13 windling sheet *winding sheet, shroud*

74

The Cruel Mother

1 There lives a lady in London,
      All alone and alone ee
  She's gane wi bairn to the clerk's son.
      Down by the green wood sae bonnie

2 She's taen her mantle her about,
  She's gane aff to the gude green wood.

3 She's set her back untill an oak,
  First it bowed and then it broke.

4 She's set her back untill a tree,
  Bonny were the twa boys she did bear.

5 But she took out a little pen-knife,
  And she parted them and their sweet life.

6 She's aff untill her father's ha;
  She was the lealest maiden that was amang them a'.

7 As she lookit oure the castle wa,
  She spied twa bonnie boys playing at the ba.

8 'O if these two babes were mine,
  They should wear the silk and the sabelline!'

9 'O mother dear, when we were thine,
  We neither wore the silks nor the sabelline.

10 'But out ye took a little pen-knife,
  And ye parted us and our sweet life.

11 'But now we're in the heavens hie,
  And ye've the pains o hell to drie.'

6 lealest *truest*
8 sabelline *sable* · 11 drie *suffer*

75

Marie Hamilton

1 Word's gane to the kitchen,
    And word's gane to the ha,
That Marie Hamilton gangs wi bairn
    To the hichest Stewart of a'.

2 He's courted her in the kitchen,
    He's courted her in the ha,
He's courted her in the laigh cellar,
    And that was warst of a'.

3 She's tyed it in her apron
    And she's thrown it in the sea;
Says, Sink ye, swim ye, bonny wee babe!
    You'l neer get mair o me.

4 Down then cam the auld queen,
    Goud tassels tying her hair:
'O Marie, where's the bonny wee babe
    That I heard greet sae sair?'

5 'There never was a babe intill my room,
    As little designs to be;
It was but a touch o my sair side,
    Come oer my fair bodie.'

6 'O Marie, put on your robes o black,
    Or else your robes o brown,
For ye maun gang wi me the night,
    To see fair Edinbro town.'

7 'I winna put on my robes o black,
    Nor yet my robes o brown;
But I'll put on my robes o white,
    To shine through Edinbro town.'

2 laigh *low*

8 When she gaed up the Cannogate,
     She laughd loud laughters three;
  But whan she cam down the Cannogate
     The tear blinded her ee.

9 When she gaed up the Parliament stair,
     The heel cam aff her shee;
  And lang or she cam down again
     She was condemnd to dee.

10 When she cam down the Cannogate,
     The Cannogate sae free,
  Many a ladie lookd oer her window,
     Weeping for this ladie.

11 'Ye need nae weep for me,' she says,
     'Ye need nae weep for me;
  For had I not slain mine own sweet babe,
     This death I wadna dee.

12 'Bring me a bottle of wine,' she says,
     'The best that eer ye hae,
  That I may drink to my weil-wishers,
     And they may drink to me.

13 'Here's a health to the jolly sailors,
     That sail upon the main;
  Let them never let on to my father and mother
     But what I'm coming hame.

14 'Here's a health to the jolly sailors,
     That sail upon the sea;
  Let them never let on to my father and mother
     That I cam here to dee.

15 'Oh little did my mother think,
     The day she cradled me,
  What lands I was to travel through,
     What death I was to dee.

16 'Oh little did my father think,
    The day he held up me,
What lands I was to travel through,
    What death I was to dee.

17 'Last night I washd the queen's feet,
    And gently laid her down;
And a' the thanks I've gotten the nicht
    To be hangd in Edinbro town!

18 'Last nicht there was four Maries,
    The nicht there 'l be but three;
There was Marie Seton, and Marie Beton,
    And Marie Carmichael, and me.'

18 Maries *maids-of-honour*

76

Earl Richard

1 Earl Richard is a hunting gane
    As hard as he could ride
His hunting horn about his neck
    An his braid sword by his side
    An his braid sword by his side

2 But as he was hunting
    Down by Charter's hall
He stopped at his trew loves gate
    And there he began to call

3 He stopped at his trew love's gate
        And he tinklit at the ring
    There was nane sae ready as lady Margaret hersel
        For to let Earl Richard in

4 Light down, licht doun Earl Richard she said
        An cum my bower within
    And ye shall have cheer and charcoal clear
        An candles for to burn

5 I canna licht down Earl Richard he said
        Nor I winna licht doun at aw
    For a lady fairer than ten o thee
        Is to meet me at Richard's haw

6 He loutit owr his saddle bow
        For to kiss her lips sae sweet
    But little thought he o that pen knife
        Wherewith she wound him deep

7 Why wound you me sae deep lady
        Why wound you me sae sair
    For there's no a man in aw Scotland
        Loves a fause woman mair

8 She carried him into her bower
        An laid him on a bed
    And painfullie she watched him
        Until he was dead

9 She called on her waiting maids
        Twa hours ere it was day
    Sayand – I hae a dead Squire in my bower
        And I wiss he were awa

4 cheer *food*
6 loutit *leaned*

10 Silver then shall be your hire
      And gold shall be your fee
  And I will gang alang wi you
      And keep you company

11 They sadled him and bridled him
      As he was wont to ride
  Wi his hunting horn about his neck
      An his braid sword by his side

12 The tane o them tuke his head
      And the ither tuke his feet
  Until thay came to yon wan water
      An they threw him in the deep

13 Now lie ye there Earl Richard she said
      Till the bluid cums frae your bane
  An the lady fairer than ten o me
      Will weary till you gang hame

14 But as she was walking hame
      A wee bird on a tree
  Said Gang hame gang hame ye fause lady
      An pay your servants' fee

15 Cum down Cum doun my bonnie wee bird
      Cum doun and speak to me
  For I hae a cage o beaten gold
      Whaurin I will pit thee

16 It's ye maun keep your golden cage
      An I will keep my tree
  For as ye hae did to your trew luve
      So wud you do to me

17 Ye wad cut aff my little head
      Throw my body in the sea
  An as ye said to your trew luve
      Sa wad ye say to me

18 Gae bring to me my bendit bow
  And set it at my ee
  And I'll gar this bonnie wee bird
  Cum down and speak to me

19 Before that ye get your bow bent
  And right set at your ee
  I'll be far far in yon forest
  Telland ill tales on thee

77

Lord Thomas and Lady Margeret

1 Lord Thomas he was a guid Lord's son
  Lady Margeret she lo'ed him weel
  An' for the sake o' guid Lord Thomas
  Lady Margeret she's gane wild

2 He called up his merry men a'
  By ane by twa an' by three
  Sayin' gae an' hunt this wild woman
  Mony a mile frae me

3 They hunted her heigh an' they hunted her low
  They hunted her oure the plain
  Till the petticoat o' scarlet Lady Margeret wore
  Coud ne'er be worn again

4 She leuked heigh an' she leuked laigh
  An' she leuked roun' again
  An' there she saw a braw scots Lord
  Come ridin' owre the plain

4 laigh *low*

5 Some help some help my guid lord she said
   Some help pray gie tae me
I am a leddy that's deeplie in love
   An' banish'd frae my ain kintrie

6 Nae help nae help leddy Margeret he said
   Nae help I gie tae the
Till ye forsake a' the men in the warld
   My ain wedded bride tae be

7 I'll forsake a' the men in the warld
   By ane by twa an' by three
I will forsake a' the men in the warld
   Your ain wedded bride tae be

8 Lady Margeret sat in her bour window
   A silken seam sew'd she
An' there she saw her guid lord Thomas
   In beggar's garb was he

9 Some help some help leddy Margeret
   Some help come shew tae me
Or wi' my braid sword I'll kill your Lord
   An' my ain wedded bride ye'll be

10 O gude forbid Lord Thomas she said
   That ony sic thing shou'd be
For I'v twenty casks in my cellar
   An' ye'se taste them a' wi' me

11 She called for her butler boy
   Tae draw her a pint o' wine
An' wi' her fingers lang an' sma'
   She steer'd the poison in

12 She put it tae her rosie cheeks
        Syne tae her dimple'd chin
    She put it tae her rubbie lips
        But ne'er a drap gaed in

13 He put it tae his rosie cheeks
        Syne tae his dimple'd chin
    He put it tae his rubbie lips
        An' the rank poison gaed in

14 Tak' awa your wine leddy Margeret
        For o' it I am wearie
    An' sae was I o' your hounds Lord Thomas
        Whan ye hunted them after me

15 But I will burry you as decentlie she said
        As ony o' your kin
    An' I will tell my ain wedded Lord
        That you are my sister's son

78

Lord Ronald

1 'Oh, where have you been to, Lord Ronald my son?
        Oh, where have you been to, my handsome young man?'
    'I've been to the woods, mother, make my bed soon,
        For I'm weary o huntin' an fain wad lie doon.'

2 'What got ye for dinner, Lord Ronald my son?
        What got ye for dinner, my handsome young man?'
    'I got eels boiled in broth, mother, make my bed soon,
        For I'm weary o' huntin' and fain wad lie doon.'

3 'Oh, where did they come from, Lord Ronald my son?
        Oh, where did they come from, my handsome young man?'
    'From my father's black ditch, mother, make my bed soon,
        For I'm weary o' huntin' and fain wad lie doon.'

4 'Oh, where are your bloodhounds, Lord Ronald my son?
    Oh, where are your bloodhounds, my handsome young man?'
'They swelled and they died, mother, make my bed soon,
    For I'm weary o' huntin' and fain wad lie doon.'

5 'I fear you are poisoned, Lord Ronald my son,
    I fear you are poisoned, my handsome young man.'
'Oh yes, I am poisoned, mother, make my bed soon,
    For I'm sick at the heart, and fain wad lie doon.'

6 'What'll ye leave to your father, Lord Ronald my son?
    What'll ye leave to your father, my handsome young man?'
'My lands and my gold, mother, make my bed soon,
    For I'm weary o' huntin' and fain wad lie doon.'

7 'What'll ye leave to your brother, Lord Ronald my son?
    What'll ye leave to your brother, my handsome young man?'
'My gold watch and chain, mother, make my bed soon,
    For I'm weary o' huntin' and fain wad lie doon.'

8 'What'll ye leave to your sweetheart, Lord Ronald my son?
    What'll ye leave to your sweetheart, my handsome young man?'
'I'll leave her a rope, and a high gallows tree,
    And let her hang there for the poisonin' o' me.'

79

Bonny Barbara Allan

1 It was in and about the Martinmas time,
    When the green leaves were a falling,
That Sir John Graeme, in the West Country,
    Fell in love with Barbara Allan.

2 He sent his men down through the town,
  To the place where she was dwelling:
'O haste and come to my master dear,
  Gin ye be Barbara Allan.'

3 O hooly, hooly rose she up,
  To the place where he was lying,
And when she drew the curtain by,
  'Young man, I think you're dying.'

4 'O it's I'm sick, and very, very sick,
  And 't is a' for Barbara Allan:'
'O the better for me ye's never be,
  Tho your heart's blood were a spilling.

5 'O dinna ye mind, young man,' said she,
  'When ye was in the tavern a drinking,
That ye made the healths gae round and round,
  And slighted Barbara Allan?'

6 He turnd his face unto the wall,
  And death was with him dealing:
'Adieu, adieu, my dear friends all,
  And be kind to Barbara Allan.'

7 And slowly, slowly raise she up,
  And slowly, slowly left him,
And sighing said, she coud not stay,
  Since death of life had reft him.

8 She had not gane a mile but twa,
  When she heard the dead-bell ringing,
And every jow that the dead-bell geid,
  It cry'd, Woe to Barbara Allan!

3 hooly *slowly*
7 reft *bereft*
8 dead-bell *passing bell* · jow *stroke*

9 'O mother, mother, make my bed!
   O make it saft and narrow!
   Since my love died for me to-day,
   I'll die for him to-morrow.'

80

The Blue Flowers and the Yellow

1 'This seven long years I've courted a maid,'
    As the sun shines over the valley
  'And she neer would consent for to be my bride.'
    Among the blue flowers and the yellow

2 'O Jamie, O Jamie, I'll learn you the way
   How your innocent love you'll betray.

3 'If you will give to the bell-man a groat,
   And he'll toll you down a merry night-wake.'

4 Now he has given the bell-man a groat,
   And he has tolld him down a merry night-wake.

5 'It's I must go to my true-love's wake,
   For late last night I heard he was dead.'

6 'Take with you your horse and boy,
   And give your true lover his last convoy.'

7 'I'll have neither horse nor boy,
   But I'll go alone, and I'll mourn and cry.'

8 When that she came to her true-love's hall,
   Then the tears they did down fall.

3 groat *small silver coin* · night-wake *night watch over a
dead body*
6 convoy *escort (in the funeral procession)*

9 She lifted up the sheets so small,
   He took her in his arms and he threw her to the wa.

10 'It's let me go a maid, young Jamie,' she said,
   'And I will be your bride, and to-morrow we'll be wed.'

11 'If all your friends were in this bower,
   You should not be a maid one quarter of an hour.

12 'You came here a maid meek and mild,
   But you shall go home both marryd and with child.'

13 He gave to her a gay gold ring,
   And the next day they had a gay wedding.

9 small *finely textured*

81

Glenlogie

1 There was mony a braw noble cum to our king's ha,
  But the bonnie Glenlogie was the flower o them a';
  An the young ladye Jeanye, sae gude an sae fair,
  She fancyd Glenlogie aboon a' that were there.

2 She speered at his footman that rode by his side
  His name an his surname an whare he did bide:
  'He bides a[t] Glenlogie whan he is at hame,
  He is of the gay Gordons, an John is his name.'

3 'Oh, Logie, Glenlogie, I'll tell you my mind;
  My luve is laid on you, O wad ye prove kind!'
  He turned him about, as the Gordons do a',
  'I thank [you], fair ladye, but I'm promised awa.'

4 She called on her maidens her hands for to take,
An the rings on her fingers she did them a' break:
'Oh, Logie, Glenlogie! Oh, Logie!' said she,
'Gin I get na Glenlogie, I'm sure I will die.'

5 'O hold your tongue, daughter, an weep na sae sair,
For ye'll get Drumfindlay, his father's young heir.'
'O hold your tongue, father, an let me alane,
Gin I get na Glenlogie, I winna hae ane.'

6 Her father wrote a broad letter wi speed,
And ordered his footman to run and ride;
He wrote a broad letter, he wrote it wi skill,
An sent it to Glenlogie, who had dune her the ill.

7 The first line that he read, a light laugh gae he;
The next line that he read, the tear filld his ee:
'O what a man am I, an hae I a maik,
That such a fine ladye shoud die for my sake?

8 'Ye'll saddle my horse, an ye'll saddle him sune,
An, when he is saddled, bring him to the green:'
His horse was na saddled an brocht to the green,
When Glenlogie was on the road three miles his lane.

9 When he came to her father's, he saw naething there
But weeping an wailing an sobbing fu sair:
O pale an wan was she when Logie gaed in,
But red an ruddie grew she when Logie gaed ben.

10 'O turn, Ladye Jeany, turn ye to your side,
For I'll be the bridegroom, an ye'll be the bride:'
It was a blythe wedding as ever I've seen,
An bonny Jeany Melville was scarce seventeen.

7 maik *equal*
8 his lane *alone*
9 ben *to the inner room*

82

The Twa Corbies

1 As I was walking all alane,
  I heard twa corbies making a mane;
  The tane unto the t'other say,
  'Where sall we gang and dine to-day?'

2 'In behint yon auld fail dyke,
  I wot there lies a new slain knight;
  And naebody kens that he lies there,
  But his hawk, his hound, and lady fair.

3 'His hound is to the hunting gane,
  His hawk to fetch the wild-fowl hame,
  His lady's ta'en another mate,
  So we may mak our dinner sweet.

4 'Ye'll sit on his white hause-bane,
  And I'll pike out his bonny blue een;
  Wi ae lock o his gowden hair
  We'll theek our nest when it grows bare.

5 'Mony a one for him makes mane,
  But nane sall ken where he is gane;
  Oer his white banes, when they are bare,
  The wind sall blaw for evermair.'

1 corbies *ravens, crows* · making a mane *talking together*
2 fail dyke *turf wall*
4 hause-bane *collar bone* · pike *peck* · theek *thatch*
5 makes mane *laments*

83

The Thrie Ravens

1 Thrie ravens sat upon a tree
   Hey doun hey derrie day
   Thrie ravens sat upon a trie
   Hey down
   Thrie ravens sat upon a trie
   And they were black as black could be
   And sing lay doo-an la doo-an day

2 The middlemaist ane said to its mate
   O quher'll we our dinner get

3 O doun into yon green grass field
   Thare lies a Squire baith killed and dead

4 His horse was standing by his side
   An thought he soud get on and ride

5 His hounds war standing by his feet
   An lick't his sairs they war so deep

6 Thare cam a lady fu o woe
   As big wi child as she could go

7 She streach't hersel doun by his side
   An for the luve o him she died

8 He was burried in Sanct Mary's kirk
   An she was burried in Sanct Mary's quier

9 Out o his grave thare grew a fir
   And out o hers a lily fair

8 quier *choir* · 10 cuist *tied*

10 They grew till they grew to the kirk top
     And there they cuist a true love knot

11 O dinna ye think but their love was true
     When out of their graves sic flowers do grow

Notes

ABBREVIATIONS

Buchan's *Ballads*: *Ancient Ballads and Songs of the North of Scotland*, ed. Peter Buchan (Edinburgh 1828)

Buchan's *Gleanings*: *Gleanings of Scotch, English, and Irish scarce old Ballads chiefly tragical and historical*, ed. Peter Buchan (Peterhead 1825)

Child: *The English and Scottish Popular Ballads*, ed. Francis James Child (Boston 1882–98).

Crawfurd: *Andrew Crawfurd's Collection of Ballads and Songs*, ed. Emily B. Lyle (Edinburgh 1975–94).

Greig-Duncan: *The Greig-Duncan Folk Song Collection*, ed. Patrick Shuldham-Shaw, Emily B. Lyle, Peter Hall, Andrew R. Hunter, Adam McNaughtan, Elaine Petrie and Sheila Douglas (Aberdeen and Edinburgh 1981–).

Percy's *Reliques*: *Reliques of Ancient English Poetry: consisting of Old Heroic Ballads, Songs, and other pieces of our Earlier Poets, together with some few of later date*, ed. Thomas Percy (London 1765).

Ramsay's *Tea-Table Miscellany*: *The Tea-Table Miscellany, or a collection of Choice Songs, Scots and English*, ed. Allan Ramsay (Edinburgh, 1763 edition).

Scott's *Minstrelsy*: *Minstrelsy of the Scottish Border, consisting of Historical and Romantic Ballads collected in the Southern Counties of Scotland, with a few of modern date, founded upon local tradition*, ed. Walter Scott (vols. 1–2 Kelso 1802; vol. 3 Edinburgh 1803; and later editions).

Notes

The following are in the Houghton Library, Harvard: the Harris MS (25241.17*), the Kinloch MSS (25242.12*), the Laing MS (25241.43*) and a copy of the Motherwell MS *Note-Book*, the original of which was formerly at Pollok House, Glasgow (25242.16*). The others are at various locations in Scotland: the Glenbuchat MSS in Aberdeen University Archive (2181/1–4), the Macmath MS in the Hornel Library, Kirkcudbright, the Motherwell MS in Glasgow University Library (Murray 501), the Jamieson-Brown MS in Edinburgh University Library (La.III.473) and William Tytler's Brown MS and Alexander Fraser-Tytler's Brown MS in the National Library of Scotland (Acc. 10611). For further details of the manuscripts, see E. B. Lyle, 'Child's Scottish Harvest', *Harvard Library Bulletin* 25 (1977), 125–54.

1 The Battle of Otterburn

Child No 161 'The Battle of Otterburn' C, from Scott's *Minstrelsy* (1833), 1.345, which consists of the version published in *Ancient and Modern Scottish Songs*, ed. David Herd (1776), 1.153, supplemented from three other sources. Two of the copies used were received from James Hogg who had collected them from an old man and a woman at the head of Ettrick Forest (Child 4.499). This account of the battle of Otterburn, fought in Northumberland in 1388, is told from the Scottish standpoint; another version (Child A) tells it from the English angle.

2 Kinmont Willie

Child No 186 'Kinmont Willie', from Scott's *Minstrelsy* (1802), 1.111. William Armstrong, known as Will of Kinmont or Kinmonth, had been taken prisoner by the English during a time of truce, and on 13 April 1596 several hundred Scottish horsemen led by Sir Walter Scott of Branxholm, laird of Buccleuch, crossed the border into England and rescued him from Carlisle Castle. This is the sole text of the ballad and it incorporates Scott's revisions. Lord Scroop was Warden of the West-Marches of England and Mr Salkeld was his representative at the time of truce. Haribee (verse 1) was the place of execution outside Carlisle and Branxholm Hall (verse 8) is southwest of Hawick.

Liddel Water (verses 3–4) is on the Scottish/English border, the River Eden (verse 26) runs just north of Carlisle, and the Debatable Land (verse 20) was 'a tract of country between the Rivers Esk and Sark whose nationality was not officially established until 1552'. See James Reed, *The Border Ballads* (London 1973; reprint Stocksfield 1991), p. 42, and map, pp. 14–15. This book gives useful background for the ballads set in the Borders.

3 Johnie Armstrang

Child No 169 'Johnie Armstrong' C, from *The Ever Green*, ed. Allan Ramsay (1724), 2.190, 'copied from a gentleman's mouth of the name of Armstrang, who is the 6th generation from this John'. Gilnockie is on the River Esk near Langholm. Whatever the rights and wrongs of the power of the Armstrongs on the Border, there is no doubt in terms of the ballad itself that the king has broken his word and is condemned for this although he has the authority to have Armstrong and all his men executed.

4 The Battle o' Harlaw

Child No 163 'The Battle of Harlaw'. *Greig-Duncan* 1.303–304, No 112 B, with tune, collected by James B. Duncan from Isaac Troup on 11 September 1907. The battle was fought in Aberdeenshire in 1411. On the ballad and history, see David Buchan, 'History and Harlaw' in E. B. Lyle, *Ballad Studies* (Cambridge 1976), pp. 29–40, and review by Hamish Henderson in *Tocher* 27 (1977), p. 186.

5 Johnnie o' Braidiesleys

Child No 114 'Johnie Cock'. *Greig-Duncan* 2.242, No 250 N, with tune, sent to Gavin Greig by David Rorie in April 1909. The previous ballads deal, however personally, with events at the national level, but there are also ballads that tell of episodes of small-scale raiding and rescue. Here the theft is the poaching of the king's deer in which the sympathy of the ballad lies with the poacher as in the English cycle of Robin Hood ballads. This episode has not been identified historically and it is located in different places in different versions.

6 Sir Patrick Spens

Child No 58 'Sir Patrick Spens' H, from Scott's *Minstrelsy*

(1803), 3.64, 'taken from two MS. copies, collated with several verses recited by the editor's friend, Robert Hamilton, Esq., Advocate'. The ballad first appears in the late eighteenth century, but the only time when an embassy was sent to bring the daughter of the king of Norway to Scotland was 1290 and so the historical event that is touched on in the ballad is placeable at that time. As a matter of history, the young princess, the 'Maid of Norway' as she was called, died in Orkney, and her death left the way open to conflicting claims to the throne.

7 The Bonny Earl of Murray

Child No 181 'The Bonny Earl of Murray', from Ramsay's *Tea-Table Miscellany* (1763), p. 356. The historical reference of this lament is to the reign of James VI, when James Stewart, Earl of Moray, who had apparently been associated with the Earl of Bothwell in an assault on Holyrood House, was killed at Donibristle in Fife by the Earl of Huntly and his party in February 1592.

8 Edom of Gordon

Child No 178 'Captain Car, or, Edom o Gordon' D, from *'Edom of Gordon,' an ancient Scottish Poem. Never before printed*, Glasgow, printed and sold by Robert and Andrew Foulis, Glasgow, 1755; 'as preserved in the memory of a lady'. In November 1571, in the reign of Mary, Queen of Scots, Sir Adam Gordon, the queen's lieutenant deputy in the north, burnt the castle of Alexander Forbes, destroying his wife, children and servants. The castle was in Aberdeenshire at Towie, or alternatively at Corgarff, fifteen miles west of Towie, but this version of the ballad has transferred the scene to Berwickshire and identified the place as the house of Rodes, near Duns.

9 The Bonnie Hoose o Airlie

Child No 199 'The Bonnie House o Airlie'. *Tocher* No. 21 (1976), pp. 174–5, with tune, recorded by Hamish Henderson from Belle Stewart. The Earl of Argyle destroyed Airlie House, the home of the Earl of Airlie, in 1640. In the ballad, the events of this time have been conflated with those of the '45 rebellion in the next century.

10 The Baron of Brackley
Child No 203 'The Baron of Brackley'. Recording by Norman
Buchan in the archive of the School of Scottish Studies (SA 1964/
67 A6) from Anne Neilson, Glasgow, who learnt it from revival
singers, notably Robin Hall; this version was launched on the folk
scene by Hamish Henderson. There were episodes in 1592 and
1666 that provide an appropriate setting for this ballad, but the
strong story-line is not known to reflect any actual historical
event. Brackley is in Deeside, near Ballater. The reference in the
last verse is to Glen Tanar; the lady is advising Inverey how to get
away.

11 The Gaberlunzie-Man
Child No 279 'The Jolly Beggar', appendix 'The Gaberlunyie-
Man'. Broadside in the National Library of Scotland, BL.el.1055,
reprinted here for the first time. The entire heading runs: AN
EXCELLEN BALLADT, / INTITULED / The Gaberlunzie-Man'. The 'z'
in the last word represents the older letter yogh and is pronounced
'y'. Some omitted letters have been added in square brackets and
at 6.3, 11.4 and 17.2 corrections have been made in the words
printed as 'Ttade', 'Graberlounzie' and 'Tewnty'. Although
undated, this broadside appears to be of the eighteenth century
or earlier, and it provides a missing link in our understanding of
the transmission of this ballad. The earliest dated version was
published in *The Tea-Table Miscellany*, ed. Allan Ramsay in 1724,
and the version there, which was often reprinted, ends with a
conversation between the couple shortly after the daughter's
departure has been discovered. The return years later, however,
occurs in many versions recorded from oral tradition and we can
now see that this form of the ballad existed early in the tradition
and may well have preceded the *Tea-Table* version which would
then be seen as a truncated form of the story. The supposed
beggar who turns out to be a wealthy gentleman has been
associated, though not in the wording of the ballad itself, with
James V.

12 Donald of the Isles
Child No 226 'Lizie Lindsay' C, from the Kinloch MSS, 1.253,
from Mrs Bouchart, Dundee.

13 Johny Faa, the Gypsy Laddie
Child No 200 'The Gypsy Laddie' A, from Ramsay's *Tea-Table Miscellany* (1763), p. 427. In this ballad as in the last one, the woman leaves home in company with a stranger. Here the mention of 'the glamer' in the first verse suggests that she did not have control over her actions, but other verses imply that she was very willing. Some versions of the ballad refer to her as the 'Earl of Cassillis' lady' and she has been identified traditionally as Lady Jean Hamilton who married the sixth Earl of Cassillis in 1621 although there is no direct historical evidence. This tradition locates the ballad at Culzean Castle, south-west of Ayr. See Sigrid Rieuwerts, 'The Historical Moorings of "The Gypsy Laddie": Johnny Faa and Lady Cassillis' in *The Ballad and Oral Literature*, ed. Joseph Harris (Cambridge, Mass., 1991), 78–96.

14 The Gowans Sae Gay
Child No 4 'Lady Isabel and the Elf-Knight' A, from Buchan's *Ballads* (1828), 1.22. This ballad is known in widely different forms in Scotland and has an international currency. In all cases, the lady turns the tables on the mass murderer who intends to make her his next victim. In the version given here, the stranger is a supernatural being, and the lady has some skill in magic that she uses to oppose him.

15 The Wind Hath Blown My Plaid Away
Child No 2 'The Elfin Knight' A, from a broadside of c. 1670 headed 'A proper new ballad entituled The Wind hath blown my Plaid away, or, A Discourse betwixt a young [Wo]man and the Elphin Knight' in the Pepys Library, Magdalene College, Cambridge. Nos 15–18 deal with riddle contests between a mortal and a supernatural being or between two mortals. They are discussed by David Buchan in 'Wit-Combat Ballads' in *Narrative Folksong: New Directions* ed. Carol L. Edwards and Kathleen E. B. Manley (Boulder, Colo., 1985), pp. 380–400.

16 The Earl of Rosslyn's Daughter
Child No 46 'Captain Wedderburn's Courtship' B, from the Kinloch MSS, 1.83, from Mary Barr, Clydesdale.

17 The Unco Knicht's Wouing
Child No 1 'Riddles Wisely Expounded'. *Crawfurd*, 1.113–114,
No 45, from Mary Macqueen (Mrs Storie); this is Child's C
version.

18 The Fause Knicht
Child No 3 'The Fause Knight upon the Road'. *Crawfurd*, 1.77,
No 31, from Mary Macqueen (Mrs Storie), who learnt it from 'a
Galloway woman named Mrs Dole or Doll'. This is Child's A
version. The false knight is the devil.

19 The Daemon Lover
Child No 243 'James Harris (The Daemon Lover)' F, from
Scott's *Minstrelsy* (1812), 2.427, 'taken down from the recitation
of Walter Grieve by William Laidlaw'.

20 Burd Ellen
Child No 63 'Child Waters' B, from the Jamieson-Brown MS,
fol. 22, from Anna Gordon (Mrs Brown).

21 The Place Where My Love Johnny Dwells
Child No 218 'The False Lover Won Back' B, from *Traditional
Ballad Airs* ed. William Christie (1876–81), 1.144, 'from the
recitation of a woman born in Buchan'.

22 Young Bicham
Child No 53 'Young Beichan' A, from the Jamieson-Brown MS,
fol. 13, from Anna Gordon (Mrs Brown).

23 Hind Horn
Child No 17 'Hind Horn' A, from the Motherwell MS, p. 106,
from Mrs King, Kilbarchan. There is a medieval romance, 'Hind
Horn', with the same narrative line.

24 Katharine Jaffray
Child No 221 'Katharine Jaffray' A, from the Herd MSS, 1.61.
Scott's poem 'Lochinvar' was modelled on this ballad.

25 Lord Thomas and Fair Annie
Child No 62 'Fair Annie' A, from Scott's *Minstrelsy* (1802),
2.102, 'chiefly from the recitation of an old woman residing near

Kirkhill, in West Lothian'.

26 Wee Messgrove

Child No 81 'Little Musgrave and Lady Barnard' G, from the Motherwell MS, p. 643, taken down by Thomas Macqueen from Mrs McConechie, Kilmarnock, and copied by Motherwell. Although the ballad was widely known in Scotland and has remained current there up to the present, it appears to be of English origin and the lines 'Ever as the lord Barnet's horn blew, / Away, Musgrave, away!' are quoted in Beaumont and Fletcher's *Knight of the Burning Pestle* dated c. 1611. The repeated blowing of the horn is one of the memorable points of the ballad; in some versions, the horn is blown by a friend of Musgrave's in warning when Lord Barnet demands silence; in others, as here, it is the lord who blows the horn, perhaps out of chivalry. The motif of the silver basin at verses 28 and 30 does not generally occur in this ballad and is probably borrowed from 'Lamkin'.

27 Bob Norris

Child No 83 'Child Maurice'. *Crawfurd*, 1.8–11, No 2, with tune, from Mary Macqueen (Mrs Storie), who learnt it from her grandmother; this is Child's C version. Motherwell notes at 19.1 in his copy of the ballad (Motherwell MS, p. 510): 'the epithet applied to the sword not remembered by the reciter; but I afterwards saw her & she mentioned it was "nutbrown",' and that word is included in the text. We have here a rare case where we can follow the work of the nineteenth-century collectors closely. Motherwell speaks of 'Mrs Storie singing the ballad over to myself' while he checked the text as sent to him by Crawfurd, and he also arranged to have Andrew Blaikie record tunes from her, including this one. This ballad tragedy of mistaken identity and jealous ferocity was made the basis of John Home's play *Douglas*, which was first produced in Edinburgh in 1756 to great acclaim.

28 Lord Thomas and Fair Annet

Child No 73 'Lord Thomas and Fair Annet' A, from Percy's *Reliques* (1765), 2.293, 'given, with some corrections, from a MS. copy transmitted from Scotland'.

29 The Twa Sisters
Child No 10 'The Twa Sisters' B, from the Jamieson-Brown MS, fol. 39, from Anna Gordon (Mrs Brown).

30 Sweet William's Ghost
Child No 77 'Sweet William's Ghost' A, from Ramsay's *Tea-Table Miscellany* (1763), p. 324.

31 The Wife of Usher's Well
Child No 79 'The Wife of Usher's Well' A, from Scott's *Minstrelsy* (1802), 2.111, 'from the recitation of an old woman residing near Kirkhill, in West Lothian'. The mother compels the powers of the supernatural to allow her dead sons to return by the force of her grief and the curse she lays, although they can return only as ghosts and must vanish at daybreak.

32 The Maid of Coldingham
Child No 21 'The Maid and the Palmer (The Samaritan Woman)'. Glenbuchat MSS, 2.17–18; not all the capitalisation of the original has been retained. Coldingham is in Berwickshire. In some other versions of this ballad, which occurs quite widely in Scandinavia, the man who asks for drink is Jesus and the story then has a stronger link with the biblical account (John 4) of a meeting beside a well between Jesus and the woman of Samaria. In the slightly fuller narrative in the English version, Child A, the old man mentions the woman's lover and the woman, at the point corresponding to verse 5 here, swears that she has never had a lover. The old man then says that she has sworn falsely and reveals the birth and murder of her children.

33 Clark Colven
Child No 42 'Clerk Colvill' A, from a transcript of William Tytler's Brown MS, No 13, from Anna Gordon (Mrs Brown).

34 The Great Silkie of Sule Skerry
Child No 113 'The Great Silkie of Sule Skerry', from *The Proceedings of The Society of Antiquaries of Scotland* 1 (1852), 86; 'communicated by the late Captain F. W. L. Thomas, R. N.; written down by him from the dictation of a venerable lady of Snarra Voe, Shetland'. Sule Skerry is a remote island west of Orkney. Humans are thought of as close kin of the seal people

and the fairy people and can have fruitful love relations with them. Even so, the child of the mixed union is doomed in this ballad version, and will fall victim to the human husband. Seal people and fairy people are closely associated in the legend that fits them into the biblical scheme of things, it being said that, when Lucifer was driven out of heaven and fell down to hell, some of the angels who had supported him did not fall as far as hell but landed on the earth and became fairies, or in the sea and became seal people.

35 Tam Lin

Child No 39 'Tam Lin' A, from *The Scots Musical Museum*, ed. James Johnstone (1792), p. 423, No 411; communicated by Robert Burns, who apparently combined a Borders version (Child B), which localises the happenings near Selkirk, with Ayrshire traditions known to him; see Emily B. Lyle, 'The Burns Text of "Tam Lin"', *Scottish Studies* 15 (1971), 53–65. The ballad makes reference to the belief that people, often as children, might be carried off by the fairies, and might also, if mortals were courageous enough, be recovered from them. For studies of fairy belief, see *The Good People* ed. Peter Narváez (New York and London 1991). The asterisks after verse 7 indicate an omitted verse which we can guess was of the type that begins 'He took her by the milkwhite hand/ And by the grass-green sleeve' and tells of the conception of the child, which Janet later contemplates aborting (verses 19–20).

36 Thomas the Rhymer

Child No 37 'Thomas Rymer', from Scott's *Minstrelsy* (1802), 2.251, 'from a copy obtained from a lady residing not far from Erceldoune, corrected and enlarged by one in Mrs Brown's MS'. Erceldoune is the old name for Earlston and Scott uses it here because the Thomas who was called 'Rymer', i.e. the poet, was also called Thomas of Erceldoune since he held land there. He lived in the thirteenth century and the legend of his visit to fairyland was known at least as early as the fourteenth century when it occurs in a North of England romance-prophecy called *Thomas of Erceldoune*. The ballad is first known from Mrs Brown's version. In the romance, after Thomas's meeting with the Queen of Elfland on the Eildon Hills near Melrose, 'she led him in at Eildon Hill' and took him to Elfland. When she eventually brings him back to earth she offers him a choice of whether to 'harp or carp', i.e. to be either a musician or a poet, and when he chooses the power of 'carping', she gives him the gift of truth which will make him an inspired seer-poet. Prophecies ascribed to Thomas the Rhymer, or 'True Thomas', were well known in Scotland for centuries. At 17.4 'thee' is added.

37 King Orpheus

Child No 19 'King Orfeo'. Printed from Patrick Shuldham-Shaw, 'The Ballad "King Orfeo"', *Scottish Studies* 20 (1976), pp. 124–6; originally published in *The Shetland News* of 25 August 1894 where it is said that it was 'written down from oral recitation' by Bruce Sutherland at Gloup fishing station, North Yell, Shetland, in 1865. See Marion Stewart, 'King Orphius', *Scottish Studies* 17 (1973), 1–16, for discussion of the related Scottish lay or romance (from which the ballad title has been taken). The refrain lines are in, or are derived from, Norn, the Scandinavian language of Shetland, and may not have been understood latterly by the singers. The first line means 'The wood grows green early'.

38 Sir Colin

Child No 61 'Sir Cawline', appendix, with tune at Child 5.415, from the Harris MS, fol. 5b. The words in this manuscript were written down by Amelia Harris and the tunes by her sister Jane in 1872; the sisters had learnt this ballad from their mother who died in 1845.

39 The Twa Magicians

Child No 44 'The Twa Magicians', from Buchan's *Ballads* (1828), 1.24.

40 The Broomfield Hill

Child No 43 'The Broomfield Hill' A, from Scott's *Minstrelsy* (1803), 3.271.

41 Gil Brenton

Child No 5 'Gil Brenton' A, from the Jamieson-Brown MS, No 16, fol. 34, from Anna Gordon (Mrs Brown).

42 The Broom of Cowdenknows
Child No 217 'The Broom of Cowdenknows' G, from Scott's
Minstrelsy (1803), 3.280, 'from Ettrick Forest'.

43 The Shepherd's Dochter
Child No 110 'The Knight and Shepherd's Daughter' B, from
the Kinloch MSS, 5.255.

44 The Shepherd's Son
Child 112 'The Baffled Knight' D, from *Ancient and Modern Scots Songs*, ed. David Herd (1769), p. 328.

45 Earl of Errol
Child No 231 'The Earl of Errol' D, from Buchan's *Gleanings* (1825), p. 158. The ballad, although it may embroider upon history, has a basis in fact in a dispute between the tenth Earl of Errol, Gilbert Hay, and his countess, Lady Catherine Carnegy, whom he married in January 1658. The claimed impotence of the Earl was matter of public gossip in February of the following year. Errol lies between Perth and Dundee, on the north bank of the Tay.

46 Lord Jamie Douglas
Child No 204 'Jamie Douglas' G, from the Motherwell MS, p. 345. James, second Marquis of Douglas, and Lady Barbara Erskine, the eldest daughter of John, Earl of Mar, were married in 1670 and formally separated in 1681. The marquis's chamberlain, William Lawrie, Tutor of Blackwood, was blamed for stirring up trouble between them. The earliest record of the ballad is in the 1776 edition of David Herd's *Ancient and Modern Scottish Songs*.

47 The Laird o' Drum
Child No 236 'The Laird o Drum'. *Greig-Duncan* 4.252–253, No 835 C, collected by Gavin Greig from John McAllan, September 1907. Drum is a castle a few miles west of Peterculter in Aberdeenshire and the laird of the ballad was Alexander Irvine of Drum who married Lady Mary Gordon, daughter of the Marquis of Huntly, in 1643, and 'a pretty and youthful girl', Margaret Coutts, in 1681 or 1682, when he was sixty-two. See Jonathan Forbes Leslie, *Irvines of Drum* (1909), pp. 129–130.

The ballad is not known before the nineteenth century.

48 The Cooper of Fife
Child No 277 'The Wife Wrapt in Wether's Skin' C, from *The Book of Scottish Song*, ed. Alexander Whitelaw (1844), p. 333.

49 Get Up and Bar the Door
Child No 275 'Get Up and Bar the Door', from *The Ancient and Modern Scots Songs*, ed. David Herd (1769), p. 330.

50 Our Goodman
Child No 274 'Our Goodman' A, from the Herd MSS, 1.140.

51 The Farmer's Curst Wife
Child No 278 'The Farmer's Curst Wife' B, from the Macmath MS, p. 96, from Miss Jane Webster, Crossmichael, Kirkcudbrightshire, 27 August 1892.

52 Bog o' Gight
Child No 209 'Geordie'. *Greig-Duncan* 2.223–224, No 249 A, with tune, collected by Gavin Greig from John McAllan, September 1907. 'Bog o' Gight' or 'Bogygeich' Castle, which is now called Castle Gordon, is near Fochabers, Moray. There may possibly be a connection with an episode in 1554 when George Gordon, fourth earl of Huntly, was threatened with death and eventually fined for failing to execute a commission against a Highland robber, but the connection would be a remote one, and the ballad seems to be better regarded as a free-standing romantic tale. 21.4, 22.2 emended from 'Or' and 'she wasna''.

53 The Laird o Logie
Child No 182 'The Laird o Logie' A, from Scott's *Minstrelsy* (1833), 3.128, 'as recited by a gentleman residing near Biggar'. The incident took place in the reign of James VI in August 1592 when the king and the queen, Anne of Denmark, were residing at Dalkeith. Wemyss of Logie had been involved with the Earl of Bothwell in a conspiracy against the king and condemned to death, but, according to David Moysie's *Memoirs* as quoted by Child, 'the same night that he was examined, he escaped out by means of a gentlewoman whom he loved, a Dane, who conveyed him out of his keepers' hands, through the queen's chamber,

where his Majesty and the queen were lying in their beds, to a window in the backside of the place, where he went down upon a tow [rope], and shot three pistols in token of his onlouping [mounting his horse].'

54 Johnie Scott
Child No 99 'Johnie Scot' G, from the Motherwell MS *Note-Book*, p. 35, 'from the singing of Agnes Lyle, of Kilbarchan, 24 August, 1825'. This ballad version is examined in detail at pages 57–68 of *The Ballad Matrix* by William Bernard McCarthy (Bloomington and Indianapolis 1990) which is a study of Agnes Lyle's repertoire. Unlike the rescue in the previous ballad, there is no claim to historicity in this case, and the story is pure fantasy. The fantastic element is further developed in 55 'Lang Johnny Moir' which seems to be a related ballad.

55 Lang Johnny Moir
Child No 251 'Lang Johnny More' from Buchan's *Ballads*, 1.248.

56 The Keach i the Creel
Child No 281 'The Keach i the Creel' A, from *The Book of Scottish Ballads*, ed. Alexander Whitelaw (1845), p. 35, 'taken down from the recitation of a gentleman in Liddesdale'.

57 The Gay Goss Hawk
Child No 96 'The Gay Goshawk' A, from the Jamieson-Brown MS, No 6, pt 15, from Anna Gordon (Mrs Brown).

58 Love Gregor
Child No 76 'The Lass of Roch Royal' E, from Alexander Fraser Tytler's Brown MS, No 2, from Anna Gordon (Mrs Brown). Although the mother accuses the young woman of being a witch, it seems rather that it is the mother who is one and that her ability to mimic her son's voice at the critical juncture is more than natural.

59 The Drowned Lovers
Child No 216 'The Mother's Malison, or, Clyde's Water' C, from Buchan's *Ballads* (1828), 1.140.

60 The Dowie Dens o' Yarrow
Child No 214 'The Braes o Yarrow'. *Greig-Duncan* 2.99, No 215
A, with tune, sent to James B. Duncan by Mrs Margaret Harper,
Cluny, who had noted it from the singing of her father, James
Greig, about 1893. This ballad is known widely in Scottish
tradition. The recurrent use of the place-name in a rhyming
position has meant that, whatever variations there have been in
the story (with the lover, for example, being a gentleman rather
than a 'ploughman lad' as here), the setting has remained the
hills and dales around Yarrow Water which joins Ettrick Water
near Selkirk to form the River Tweed.

61 The Douglas Tragedy
Child No 7 'Earl Brand' B, from Scott's *Minstrelsy* (1803), 3.246,
'the copy principally used supplied by Mr Sharpe, the three last
stanzas from a penny pamphlet and from tradition'. This ballad,
which has Scandinavian analogues, is located in its Scottish form
in the same neighbourhood as the preceding ballad. According
to Scott, 'Lady Margaret is said to have been carried by her lover'
from a tower near Blackhouse Farm in Selkirkshire. Seven large
stones in the vicinity were said to mark the spot where the seven
brothers were killed, and the lovers were said to have stopped to
drink in the Douglas Burn.

62 Clerk Sanders
Child No 69 'Clerk Saunders' A, from the Herd MSS, 1.177,
2.419.

63 Lady Maisry
Child No 65 'Lady Maisry' A, from the Jamieson-Brown MS, fol.
24, from Anna Gordon (Mrs Brown).

64 The Broom o the Cathery Knowes
Child No 95 'The Maid Freed from the Gallows' B, from the
Motherwell MS, p. 290, from Mrs McCormick, 'learned in
Dumbarton'. The Scottish versions of this international ballad
are all fragmentary but the conclusion is a happy one whenever
it is present, the lover proving more true to the girl than her blood
relations. In Child D, from the north-east of Scotland, the girl
appeals finally to her love Willie and he replies:

'Ye's get a' my goud,
    And a' my well won fee,
To save ye fra the headin-hill,
    And frae the gallow-tree.'

65 The Cruel Brother
Child No 11 'The Cruel Brother' B, from the Kinloch MSS, 1.21, from Mary Barr, Clydesdale, May 1827.

66 Son David
Child No 13 'Edward'. Herschel Gower and James Porter, 'Jeannie Robertson: The Child Ballads', *Scottish Studies* 14 (1970), pp. 41–42. The incest motif found in the next three ballads has sometimes been thought to lie behind the killing in this one but the focus is on the revelation and the reason for the killing is not included in the song. Jeannie Robertson, the singer of this version, considered that David was the elder brother, that the younger brother was jealous of his rights and possessions and attacked him, and that David's killing of his brother was an act of self-defence; see James Porter, 'Jeannie Robertson's "My Son David": A Conceptual Performance Model', *Journal of American Folklore* 89 (1976), 7–26.

67 Rosianne
Child No 51 'Lizie Wan'. *Crawfurd*, 1.115–117, No 46, from Mary Macqueen (Mrs Storie); this is Child's version B.

68 Lady Jean
Child No 52 'The King's Dochter Lady Jean'. *Crawfurd*, 1.89–92, No 36, with tune, from Mary Macqueen (Mrs Storie); this is Child's version A.

69 The Broom Blooms Bonnie and Says It Is Fair
Child No 16 'Sheath and Knife' A, from the Motherwell MS, p. 286, from Mrs King, Kilbarchan, 9 February 1825. The refrain refers to 'going down to the broom' to make love; another version has 'so' instead of 'says' in the first refrain line. In a seventeenth-century form of this ballad published by Helena Mennie Shire in *Poems from Panmure House* (Cambridge 1960), pp. 12–19, an equally haunting refrain expresses the heartfelt wish of the lovers, 'If only we had not been related!'. It opens:

Ther was a sister and a brother
The sun goes to under the wood
Who most intirelie lovid othir
God give we had nevir beine sib.

70 The High Banks o Yarrow
Child No 24 'Bonnie Annie' B, from the Motherwell MS, p. 652, recorded by Thomas Macqueen from Henry French, a boy in Ayr. Other versions explain that the ship will not sail properly while a guilty person is on board and tell that, when lots are cast to find out who is responsible, the lot falls on the young woman who has been an 'undutiful daughter' in stealing from her parents.

71 Willie's Lady
Child No 6 'Willie's Lady', from Alexander Fraser-Tytler's Brown MS, a transcript of No 1, from Anna Gordon (Mrs Brown). At 24.1 'has' in Child has been emended to 'shall'.

72 Lamkin
Child No 93 'Lamkin' A, from *Popular Ballads and Songs*, ed. Robert Jamieson (1806), 1.176, from Anna Gordon (Mrs Brown).

73 The Jew's Daughter
Child No 155 'Sir Hugh, or, The Jew's Daughter' B, from Percy's *Reliques* (1765), 1.32. This ballad, which is first known from its occurrence in Scottish tradition in the eighteenth century, has its root in an outbreak of anti-semitism in Lincoln in 1255, when a number of Jews were executed for the murder of an eight-year-old Christian boy called Hugh. The name 'Mirry-land toune' is probably derived from the words 'merry Lincoln' which occur in some other versions of the ballad.

74 The Cruel Mother
Child No 20 'The Cruel Mother' D, from the Kinloch MSS, 5.103, from Miss Catherine Beattie.

75 Marie Hamilton
Child No 173 'Mary Hamilton' A, from *A Ballad Book* ed. Charles Kirkpatrick Sharpe (Edinburgh 1823), p. 18. The 'hichest Stewart' in the first verse is the king (Henry Darnley) and Marie

Hamilton is represented as one of the group of four ladies called Mary who attended Mary, Queen of Scots. They were, historically, Mary Fleming, Mary Livingston, Mary Seton and Mary Beaton and two of these names appear in the last verse. No accusation of infanticide was made against any of the Maries but a Frenchwoman in the queen's service and her lover, a royal apothecary, were hanged for murdering their child in 1563 and this incident could be the germ of the ballad. However, the ballad is not known before 1790 and could have had its starting point in a later incident that took place in Russia at the court of Peter the Great in 1719 when Mary Hamilton, a beautiful young woman who was maid-of-honour to the Empress Catherine, was beheaded for infanticide in the Czar's presence. It is not improbable that there are reminiscences of both these historical events in the ballad narrative.

76 Earl Richard

Child No 68 'Young Hunting'. *Crawfurd*, 1.93–96, No 37, with tune, from Mary Macqueen (Mrs Storie). The opening action of this ballad version forms a companion piece to the murder in 65 'The Cruel Brother'; here it is the woman on foot who kills the man on horseback rather than vice versa. A blank space left in the manuscript for a line of the ballad (6.4) probably indicates that Mary Macqueen had forgotten it (as she had forgotten the epithet for the sword in 27 'Bob Norris'; see note), and it is supplied here from the similar version sung by Agnes Lyle (Child D), where the wording of 4.3–4 and 5.1–2 runs: 'But little thocht o that penknife/ Wherewith she wound him deep.' and '"Why wounds thou me so deep, lady?/ Why stabs thou me so sore?"'. The word 'deep' in 7.1, which links with the occurrence of this word in 6.4, is also taken from this version; Mary Macqueen gave 'sair' in both 7.1 and 7.2. Some long forms of this ballad go on to tell of the finding of the earl's body and the punishment of the lady and her maidservants, but the bird's threat of coming punishment in this version makes an effective ending.

77 Lord Thomas and Lady Margeret

Child No 260 'Lord Thomas and Lady Margaret'. *Crawfurd*, Vol. 2, No 132, collected by Thomas Macqueen from an unnamed source, probably in Ayrshire.

78 Lord Ronald
Child No 12 'Lord Randal'. *Tocher*, No 14 (1974), pp. 222–223, with tune, recorded by Emily Lyle in 1974 from Mrs Haman, née Minnie Conacher, who got it from her mother who came from Perthshire.

79 Bonny Barbara Allan
Child No 84 'Bonny Barbara Allan' A, from *The Tea-Table Miscellany*, ed. Allan Ramsay (1763), p. 343. Reactions to this exceedingly widespread ballad have varied; while some have been moved to tears, others have been impatient with its hero, as Bertrand Bronson was when he remarked in the preface to the 200 tune versions of it he published in *The Traditional Tunes of the Child Ballads* that the song had shown a 'stronger will-to-live' than had its 'spineless lover'.

80 The Blue Flowers and the Yellow
Child No 25 'Willie's Lyke-Wake', from a nineteenth-century chapbook published by W. Scott, Greenock (British Library 11621.b.7: 43) reprinted at Child 4.453.

81 Glenlogie
Child No 238 'Glenlogie, or, Jean o Bethelnie' G, from the Laing MS, p. 8.

82 The Twa Corbies
Child No 26 'The Three Ravens'. This version, which was printed in Child's introduction from Scott's *Minstrelsy* (1803), 3.239, was 'communicated by C. K. Sharpe, as written down from tradition by a lady'. It is, as Child says, a 'cynical variation' on the theme of devoted love found in versions of the ballad like the one given next.

83 The Thrie Ravens
Child No 26 'The Three Ravens'. *Crawfurd*, 1.102–103, No 40, with tune, from Mary Macqueen (Mrs Storie).

Index

Child titles are included in italics when they differ from the version titles in this edition.

Baffled Knight, The, 160
Baron of Brackley, The, 61
Battle o' Harlaw, The, 44
Battle of Otterburn, The, 27
Blue Flowers and the Yellow, The, 260
Bob Norris, 105
Bog o' Gight, 178
Bonnie Annie, 237
Bonnie Hoose o Airlie, The, 59
Bonny Barbara Allan, 258
Bonny Earl of Murray, The, 54
Braes o Yarrow, The, 211
Broom Blooms Bonnie and Says It Is Fair, The, 236
Broom o the Cathery Knowes, The, 224
Broom of Cowdenknows, The, 151
Broomfield Hill, The, 142
Burd Ellen, 81
Captain Car, 55
Captain Wedderburn's Courtship, 73
Child Maurice, 105
Child Waters, 81
Clark Colven, 122
Clerk Colvill, 122
Clerk Sanders, 216
Clyde's Water, 206
Cooper of Fife, The, 170

Cruel Brother, The, 226
Cruel Mother, The, 248
Daemon Lover, The, 79
Donald of the Isles, 65
Douglas Tragedy, The, 213
Dowie Dens o' Yarrow, The, 211
Drowned Lovers, The, 206
Earl Brand, 213
Earl of Errol, The, 162
Earl of Rosslyn's Daughter, The, 73
Earl Richard, 252
Edom of Gordon, 55
Edward, 229
Elfin Knight, The, 71
Fair Annie, 96
False Lover Won Back, The, 86
Farmer's Curst Wife, The, 177
Fause Knicht, The, 78
Fause Knight upon the Road, The, 78
Gaberlunzie-Man, The, 62
Gay Goss Hawk, The, 198
Geordie, 178
Get Up and Bar the Door, 171
Gil Brenton, 144
Glenlogie, 261
Gowans Sae Gay, The, 70
Great Silkie of Sule Skerry, The, 124
High Banks o Yarrow, The, 237
Hind Horn, 91
James Harris, 79
Jamie Douglas, 164
Jean o Bethelnie, 261
Jew's Daughter, The, 246
Johnie Armstrang, 39
Johnie Cock, 48
Johnie Scott, 184
Johnnie o' Braidiesleys, 48
Johny Faa, the Gypsy Laddie, 68
Katharine Jaffray, 94
Keach i the Creel, The, 195

King Orfeo, 135
King Orpheus, 135
King's Dochter Lady Jean, The, 233
Kinmont Willie, 32
Knight and Shepherd's Daughter, The, 155
Lady Isabel and the Elf-Knight, 70
Lady Jean, 233
Lady Maisry, 220
Laird o Logie, The, 182
Laird o' Drum, The, 166
Lamkin, 242
Lang Johnny Moir, 188
Lass of Roch Royal, The, 202
Little Musgrave and Lady Barnard, 100
Lizie Lindsay, 65
Lizie Wan, 230
Lord Jamie Douglas, 164
Lord Randal, 257
Lord Ronald, 257
Lord Thomas and Fair Annet, 108
Lord Thomas and Fair Annie, 96
Lord Thomas and Lady Margeret, 255
Love Gregor, 202
Maid and the Palmer, The, 120
Maid Freed from the Gallows, The, 224
Maid of Coldingham, The, 120
Marie Hamilton, 250
Mother's Malison, The, 206
Our Goodman, 173
Place Where My Love Johnny Dwells, The, 86
Riddles Wisely Expounded, 76
Rosianne, 230
Sheath and Knife, 236
Shepherd's Dochter, The, 155
Shepherd's Son, The, 160
Sir Cawline, 137
Sir Colin, 137
Sir Hugh, 246
Sir Patrick Spens, 50
Son David, 229

Sweet William's Ghost, 115
Tam Lin, 125
Thomas Rymer, 132
Thomas the Rhymer, 132
Thrie Ravens, The, 264
Twa Corbies, The, 263
Twa Magicians, The, 140
Twa Sisters, The, 113
Unco Knicht's Wouing, The, 76
Wee Messgrove, 100
Wife of Usher's Well, The, 118
Wife Wrapt in Wether's Skin, The, 170
Willie's Lady, 239
Willie's Lyke-Wake, 260
Wind Hath Blown My Plaid Away, The, 71
Young Beichan, 88
Young Bicham, 88
Young Hunting, 252

SCHILTRON AUDIO BOOKS

Classic novels, popular fiction, short stories and memoirs, read by experienced professional actors and actresses with particular skills in storytelling and radio broadcasting.

A Scots Quair by Lewis Grassic Gibbon
Read by Eileen McCallum
Complete and Unabridged

Through the life of Chris Guthrie, struggling with conflicting loyalties to place, culture and people, Lewis Grassic Gibbon's great trilogy unforgettably depicts a changing society and an enduring land, both to be torn by the Great War and its aftermath.

'A formidably impressive reading...surefooted, versatile, spellbinding...a recording event of importance in which the author could well have taken pride' Gramophone

	Sunset Song	
SPF 320-2	8 cassettes, 10hrs 50m	£29.95
	Cloud Howe	
SPF 320-3	8 cassettes, 9hrs 16m	£29.95
	Grey Granite	
SPF 320-4	8 cassettes, 8hrs 36m	£29.95

Eileen McCallum has appeared in many notable productions on stage and screen. Her awards include the 1984 Radio Actress of the Year.

Schiltron Publishing
1 Nursery Buildings
New Lanark
Lanark
Scotland ML11 9DF
tel 0555 665645

CLOUD HOWE

LEWIS GRASSIC GIBBON

Introduced by Tom Crawford

The compelling saga of Chris Guthrie is continued in this, the middle volume of Grassic Gibbon's great trilogy *A Scots Quair*. The scene has moved to the small community of Segget, where, after Ewan's death in the First World War, Chris has come to live with her second husband, Robert Colquhoun, an idealistic and liberal minister.

Cloud Howe offers a brilliant evocation of small town life set against post-war economic hardship and the General Strike of 1926. Chris loses her baby and has to fight for a sense of her own identity in a world where only the land — and Chris herself — seem to endure with honour. Robert Colquhoun, racked by war-ruined lungs, has to wrestle with his ideals and a spiritual crisis which will eventually kill him.

Grassic Gibbon was already living in England when he wrote his great work. The incomparable artistry of *Cloud Howe* makes his self-imposed exile all the more poignant.

240 pages   ISBN 0 86241 227 7

£3.50

GREY GRANITE

LEWIS GRASSIC GIBBON

Introduced by Tom Crawford

Chris Guthrie and her son, Ewan, have come to the industrial town of Duncairn, where life is as hard as the granite of the buildings around them. These are the Depression years of the 1930s, and Chris is far from the fields of her youth in *Sunset Song*. In a society of factory owners, shopkeepers, policemen, petty clerks and industrial labourers, 'Chris Caledonia' must make her living as best she can by working in Ma Cleghorn's boarding house.

Ewan finds employment in a steel foundry and tries to lead a peaceful strike against the manufacture of armaments. In the face of violence and police brutality, his socialist idealism is forged into something harder and fiercer as he becomes a communist activist ready to sacrifice himself, his girlfriend and even the truth itself, for the cause.

Grey Granite is the last and grimmest volume of the *Scots Quair* trilogy. Chris Guthrie is one of the great characters in Scottish literature and no reader of *Sunset Song* and *Cloud Howe* should miss this last rich chapter in her tale.

234 pages   ISBN 0 86241 312 5

£3.50

CANONGATE CLASSICS

1. *Imagined Corners* Willa Muir
   ISBN 0 86241 140 8   £3.95
2. *Consider the Lilies* Iain Crichton Smith
   ISBN 0 86241 143 2   £4.99
3. *Island Landfalls: Reflections from the South Seas*
   Robert Louis Stevenson
   ISBN 0 86241 144 0   £3.95
4. *The Quarry Wood* Nan Shepherd
   ISBN 0 86241 141 6   £4.99
5. *The Story of My Boyhood and Youth* John Muir
   ISBN 0 86241 153 X   £3.99
6. *The Land of the Leal* James Barke
   ISBN 0 86241 142 4   £6.99
7. *Two Worlds* David Daiches
   ISBN 0 86241 148 3   £2.95
8. *Mr Alfred M.A.* George Friel
   ISBN 0 86241 163 7   £4.99
9. *The Haunted Woman* David Lindsay
   ISBN 0 86241 162 9   £3.95
   Memoirs of a Highland Lady vols.I&II (complete)
   Elizabeth Grant of Rothiemurchus
   ISBN 0 86241 396 6   £7.99
12. *Sunset Song* Lewis Grassic Gibbon
    ISBN 0 86241 179 3   £3.99
13. *Homeward Journey* John MacNair Reid
    ISBN 0 86241 178 5   £3.95
14. *The Blood of the Martyrs* Naomi Mitchison
    ISBN 0 86241 192 0   £4.95
15. *My First Summer in the Sierra* John Muir
    ISBN 0 86241 193 9   £3.99
16. *The Weatherhouse* Nan Shepherd
    ISBN 0 86241 194 7   £4.99
17. *Witch Wood* John Buchan
    ISBN 0 86241 202 1   £5.99
18. *Ane Satyre of the Thrie Estatis* Sir David Lindsay
    ISBN 0 86241 191 2   £4.99

19. *Cloud Howe*   Lewis Grassic Gibbon
   ISBN 0 86241 227 7   £3.50
20. *The Gowk Storm*   Nancy Brysson Morrison
   ISBN 0 86241 222 6   £3.95
21. *Tunes of Glory*   James Kennaway
   ISBN 0 86241 223 4   £3.50
22. *The Changeling*   Robin Jenkins
   ISBN 0 86241 228 5   £4.99
23. *A Childhood in Scotland*   Christian Miller
   ISBN 0 86241 230 7   £3.99
24. *The Silver Bough*   F. Marian McNeill
   ISBN 0 86241 231 5   £5.99
25. *Kidnapped*   Robert Louis Stevenson
   ISBN 0 86241 232 3   £3.99
26. *Catriona*   Robert Louis Stevenson
   ISBN 0 86241 233 1   £3.99
27. *Wild Harbour*   Ian Macpherson
   ISBN 0 86241 234 X   £3.95
28. *Linmill Stories*   Robert McLellen
   ISBN 0 86241 282 X   £4.95
29. *The Corn King and the Spring Queen*   Naomi Mitchison
   ISBN 0 86241 287 0   £6.95
30. *The Life of Robert Burns*   Catherine Carswell
   ISBN 0 86241 292 7   £5.95
31. *Dance of the Apprentices*   Edward Gaitens
   ISBN 0 86241 297 8   £5.99
32. *Fergus Lamont*   Robin Jenkins
   ISBN 0 86241 310 9   £5.99
33. *End of an Old Song*   J.D. Scott
   ISBN 0 86241 311 7   £4.95
34. *Grey Granite*   Lewis Grassic Gibbon
   ISBN 0 86241 312 5   £3.50
35. *Magnus Merriman*   Eric Linklater
   ISBN 0 86241 313 3   £4.95
36. *Diaries of a Dying Man*   William Soutar
   ISBN 0 86241 347 8   £4.95
37. *Highland River*   Neil M. Gunn
   ISBN 0 86241 358 3   £4.95

38. *The Exploits of Brigadier Gerard*
   Sir Arthur Conan Doyle
   ISBN 0 86241 341 9   £4.95
39. *The Private Memoirs and Confessions of a Justified Sinner*
   James Hogg
   ISBN 0 86241 340 0   £3.95
40. *The Devil and the Giro: Two Centuries of Scottish Stories*
   ISBN 0 86241 359 1   £7.95
41. *The Highland Lady in Ireland*
   Elizabeth Grant of Rothiemurchus
   ISBN 0 86241 361 3   £7.95
42. *Island on the Edge of the World: The Story of St Kilda*
   Charles Maclean
   ISBN 0 86241 388 5   £5.99
43. *Divided Loyalties: A Scotswoman in Occupied France*
   Janet Teissier du Cros
   ISBN 0 86241 375 3   £6.95
44. *Private Angelo*   Eric Linklater
   ISBN 0 86241 376 1   £5.95
45. *Three Scottish Poets: MacCaig, Morgan, Lochhead*
   ISBN 0 86241 400 8   £4.95
46. *The Master of Ballantrae*   Robert Louis Stevenson
   ISBN 0 86241 405 9   £4.95
47. *A Voyage to Arcturus*   David Lindsay
   ISBN 0 86241 377 X   £4.95
48. *Gillespie*   J. MacDougall Hay
   ISBN 0 86241 427 X   £6.99
49. *Listen to the Voice Selected Stories*
   Iain Crichton Smith
   ISBN 0 86241 434 2   £5.99
50. *An Autobiography*   Edwin Muir
   ISBN 0 86241 423 7   £5.99
51. *Black Lamb and Grey Falcon*   Rebecca West
   ISBN 0 86241 428 8   £9.99
52. *The Early Life of James McBey*   James McBey
   ISBN 0 86241 445 8   £5.99
53. *City of Dreadful Night*   James B.V. Thomson
   ISBN 0 86241 449 0   £4.99